Western Buddhism

294.3 KUL

Western Buddhism

Kulananda

HarperCollins*Publishers*

For my teacher, Urgyen Sangharakshita, without whose kindness, patience, wisdom and courage my life and that of countless people would have been very much diminished.

Thorsons
An Imprint of HarperCollins*Publishers*
77-85 Fulham Palace Road
Hammersmith, London W6 8JB

1160 Battery Street
San Francisco, California 94111-1213

First published by Thorsons 1997
1 3 5 7 9 10 8 6 4 2

© Kulananda, 1997

Kulananda asserts the moral right to
be identified as the author of this work

A catalogue record for this book is available
from the British Library

ISBN 0 7225 3232 6

Printed and bound in Great Britain by
Caledonian International Book Manufacturing Ltd, Glasgow

Contents

Acknowledgements

Extracts from this book have previously appeared in *The Western Buddhist Review*, *Golden Drum*, and *The Sea of Faith Journal*.

Vishvapani persuaded me to write; Ajahn Sobhano, Norman Fischer, Thubten Pende, Rev. Daishin Morgan, Kulamitra, Prajnabandhu, Ian Trome, Kamalasila, Nagabodhi, and Urgyen Sangharakshita read all or part of the manuscript and made helpful comments. Subhuti gave his time over and above the call of duty and Carole Tonkinson, at Thorsons, has been a friendly, able and constructively critical editor. Vic Burnside took the back cover photograph. I am very grateful to all of them.

The cover photograph is of a Buddhist figure at The London Buddhist Centre made by Dharmachari Chintamani.

Introduction

In April 1994 His Holiness the Dalai Lama visited the University of Michigan where he took part in a private seminar with faculty and graduate students of the Buddhist Studies programme. Donald Lopez, the resident Professor of Buddhist and Tibetan Studies, thought it would be interesting to discuss with His Holiness the current findings of Western scholarship on the origins of Mahayana Buddhism — a topic that is of great interest to the Dalai Lama and which has also been the subject of significant speculation in Buddhist studies in the last two decades.

The Dalai Lama has sometimes said that where traditional Buddhist cosmology diverges from the findings of modern Western science, the former should be discarded. Would he be as open, Professor Lopez wondered, to the findings of Western scholars of Buddhism (who call themselves 'Buddhologists') as he had been to those of Western scientists?

The traditional Mahayana Buddhist view of its own origins is that the canonical Mahayana scriptures were set forth by the Buddha at the very outset of Buddhism, 2,500 years ago, but were kept hidden for 400 years until, in the case of the *Perfection of Wisdom* literature, they were retrieved from the bottom of the ocean by the great Buddhist saint and scholar Nagarjuna. The authenticity of this vast body of scriptures, as the actual word of the Buddha, is a central claim of the traditional Mahayana schools.

Current Buddhological research, however, basing itself in archaeological, art-historical and epigraphical evidence, suggests that the Mahayana scriptures began to be composed around the beginning of the Common Era and that the Mahayana itself grew out of a disparate collection of 'cults of the book' centred on different elements of this new literature.

Three graduate students presented these ideas to the Dalai Lama who listened attentively, remaining silent at the end of the presentation and speaking only after Lopez asked him what he thought of all that had been said.

'It's something to know,' he said, evoking the Buddhist aphorism: 'Objects of knowledge are limitless'. That is, there are infinite things that can be known, and it is important to consider carefully what is truly worth knowing. He conceded that what the students had told him was interesting and that it would be good for Buddhists to have some knowledge of Western scholarship on Buddhism. However, in the end, he seemed to view Buddhist practice and Western Buddhist scholarship as ultimately irreconcilable.

He told the students that if he accepted the current Buddhological view then he would only be able to believe in the human historical form of the Buddha that appears in the world. He would not be able to believe in the archetypal Buddha figures who appear to advanced practitioners of meditation. And he could not believe in the omniscient mind of Buddhahood and its emptiness. 'If I believed what you told me,' he said, 'the Buddha would only be a nice person.'[1]

I am a second generation Western Buddhist. My teacher, an Englishman, learned much of his Buddhism in the East. I learned all of mine in the West. And just as the Dalai Lama cannot accept the findings of Western Buddhist scholarship without doing violence to his religious beliefs, so I cannot reject them — for my whole sense of what is meant by 'truth' is founded in the Western philosophical and scientific tradition. Even in these postmodern times, when notions of truth and objectivity are presented as being somehow outmoded, Western Buddhists cannot be true to themselves whilst at the same time denying the findings of serious Western scholarship.

A new kind of Buddhism is emerging in the West. One which is founded in a deep, existential engagement with Buddhist theory and practice but which, at the same time, uses the tools of Western historical scholarship to look critically at its own antecedents — both Eastern and Western.

We stand today at a highly creative juncture. The traditional, monolithic, Western orthodox religious, social and cultural consensus has largely broken down. In its place we find a vast range of volatile and fragmentary beliefs and social attitudes. At the same time we have access to world culture on a scale undreamed of even a century ago. We are free to build as our ancestors never would have thought possible. This is the milieu in which Western Buddhism is beginning to take shape.

As some of the men and women taught by myself and my contemporaries start to teach in their own right, a third and even fourth generation of Western Buddhist is coming into being. Western Buddhism has begun to take root.

This book looks at some of the doctrines and methods which Western Buddhists teach and practise. Focusing on the central Buddhist ideas of conditionality and 'emptiness', it begins with an examination of the way in which Buddhism understands the relationship between consciousness and reality — ourselves and the world. Based on the radical reassessment of this relationship that Buddhism proposes, it goes on to examine different facets of the encounter between Buddhism and Western culture as it affects the religious, cultural, social and economic lives of present-day Buddhists in Europe and North America.

Throughout, I speak in Western terms to a Western audience. In the West today one need no more speak Sanskrit, Pali, Tibetan, Chinese or Japanese to understand Buddhism than a modern Christian need speak Hebrew, Aramaic, Greek or Latin to understand Christianity. At the same time, by the fairly extensive use of footnotes, I hope to allow the more inquisitive reader to follow my tracks in the traditional canonical literature.

I am not a social scientist and this is not a phenomenological study. I have not attempted to present Western Buddhism as if I were somehow an entirely disinterested, objective observer. Indeed, from a Buddhist perspective such a claim would be judged naive, for un-Enlightened human beings (such as I am) will always only ever be able to see things from their own particular point of view. There is no cold, clear objective place to stand, uninformed by any views, whence one can propound pure 'scientific' judgements about human affairs. One's observations say as much about oneself as they do about the situation one observes: we all see things differently. I need therefore to make my perspective plain: I am a committed Buddhist and have been a member of the Western Buddhist Order since 1977. My commitment to the Buddhist path, especially as it has been elucidated by my teacher, Urgyen Sangharakshita, has long been the dominant orientation of my life and what I have to say comes from that point of view.

---

1. Donald S. Lopez, jr., 'The Buddhist and the Buddhologist', published in *Tricycle: the Buddhist Review*, New York, Summer 1995.

Chapter 1

Buddhism: a Brief Outline

IBM recently put out a billboard advertisement for their computers. From behind, it showed the head and shoulders of a Tibetan Buddhist monk as he composed an e-mail message on a computer in a temple somewhere:

to: john.paul@vatican.com.

Clearly, IBM felt no need to spell out the details of their joke. Here was the Dalai Lama, the 'Tibetan Buddhist Pope', sending a fraternal message to his Roman Catholic counterpart. Public awareness of Buddhism is much greater these days than when I first started practising it.

In the 1970s I used sometimes to hitchhike from London to Norfolk (in England) to attend Buddhist retreats. A car would pull up, I would get in, and the driver would begin a conversation.

'What do you do?'

'I'm helping to build a new Buddhist centre down in London.'

'Oh yes, Buddhists, those are the people that shave their heads and dance down the road with those drums and cymbals aren't they? Why haven't you shaved your head?'

And I'd have to explain that the people they were thinking of were Hindus, devotees of the god Krishna, and that Buddhists went about things, well, somewhat differently...

I don't hitchhike anymore but when I get into conversation with strangers these days I'm more liable to hear something like 'Oh yes, I've got a friend who goes along to a Buddhist centre. What kind of Buddhist are you?'

Even as recently as the 1950s there were probably no more than a dozen Buddhist centres in the whole Western world and most Westerners who had heard of him thought that Buddha was the name of a rather jolly, plump idol which the Chinese worshipped. Today there are many thousands of Buddhist centres in the West where Buddhism is said by some commentators to be the single fastest-growing religion.

So what did the Buddha actually teach? He taught this:

If this is, that comes to be; from the arising of this, that arises; if this is not, that does not come to be; from the stopping of this, that is stopped.[1]

That the principle of conditionality, outlined above, could be the central doctrine in a system of religious thought seems strange to those of us more familiar with a theistic approach to religion. It isn't easy for us to see the force of this idea, or to understand its liberating impact in the two central arenas of religious life: the fields of doctrine, on the one hand, and religious practice, on the other. The Buddha, however, was categorically clear about the centrality of this principle and, to paraphrase a number of quotes from a broad variety of Buddhist canonical sources[2], he put it like this:

He who sees the Principle of Conditionality[3] sees the Truth.[4]
One who sees the Truth sees the Buddha.

How strangely abstract this all sounds to Western ears. But
for the last two and a half thousand years, countless numbers
of Buddhist men and women have built their religious lives
around this teaching. It has inspired them to great acts of
devotion, renunciation, and dedicated spiritual striving, but
to us it can all sound rather hollow – abstract and uninspir-
ing. It's not at all obvious that these few words have the
potential to entirely re-orient the way in which we see the
world: to give us a completely fresh understanding of the
nature of existence and to ignite our potential for creative
transformation. Why is it that one who sees this principle
'sees the Buddha'? How can such an abstract sentence be so
spiritually significant?

Consider this example. I have a plant growing outside my
kitchen window, a shrub called *Lavatera* 'Barnsley', also
known as Tree Mallow. Its fading autumn colours still bear
a last October hint of the glories of August when the pale
green leaves provided a subtle velvet background for an
abundance of delicate, pale pink flowers. If I were to ask
someone what conditions were necessary for the *Lavatera*
'Barnsley' outside my kitchen window to flourish as it does
now, he or she would most probably begin to speak of the
need for sun and rain, for a soil adequately rich in nutri-
ments, for an absence of competing weeds and pests and so
on. This is all right and proper and one can easily see how
these conditions are the first to come to mind, but if we look
a little deeper we can see that a number of significant conditions have not been mentioned.

Despite its seeming delicacy, the *Lavatera* outside my kitchen window would probably sustain itself on soil far poorer than that in my garden. It would probably thrive in a climate much drier than the last few damp English summers have been and it is reasonably resistant to pests and encroaching weeds. What it really would not survive, outside my kitchen window, is my not liking it. Plants that I don't like get no space in this small patch of London garden. If I didn't like it, it would not be there now. An absolutely crucial condition for the continued existence of this shrub is my desire to have it where it is. My taste in flowers is a significant condition for the existence of that particular plant, and my taste in flowers, of course, is itself conditioned.

It depends, in part, on the way I was brought up, so my mother and father and their ideas of good and bad taste are important conditions for the existence of my *Lavatera*. If they had taught me differently, it would not be there. Indeed, if my mother and father had not met at a tennis party in Johannesburg in 1948, it would not be there, as I would not have been around to have planted it. If my mother had been too ill to attend a tennis party on that day, no *Lavatera*. Her good health on that day is an important condition in its life. And it follows that if my parents didn't exist in the first place, neither would our plant, so another important set of conditions for its flourishing is the history of my entire ancestry. If any of my great-great-great-great-grandparents had not met, that shrub would not be what it is today. They are, every one of them, back into the infinite depths of history, conditions for its current existence.

If I didn't live in this particular house, I would not have planted the *Lavatera* here. The fact that I share my friend Kulamitra's house with him is another condition for its existence. So if

Kulamitra and I had not met and become friends in Norwich in 1976, it wouldn't exist. In this way, Kulamitra's family history and my family history are all linked up in the network of conditions which make for the existence of the shrub.

Of course, the cultivar *Lavatera* 'Barnsley' has a history of its own. It's a plant of modern times, named after the village of Barnsley in Gloucestershire, where the garden designer Rosemary Verey created a renowned garden. Mrs. Verey spotted a mutant variant of *Lavatera* growing in a friend's garden, took a few cuttings, and grew the new plant at Barnsley House. Mrs. Verey's keen eye and her taste in plants are thus very important conditions for the existence of the shrub which grows outside my kitchen window.

In this way, a garden designer in Gloucestershire, my parents' first date in Johannesburg, my meeting up with Kulamitra in Norwich and every one of our ancestors are all interlinked in the network of conditions which support the existence of a plant in my garden.

But there is more to it than that. As we look deeper into the structure of the plant itself, we see that it is made up of a vast complex of interrelated living cells, each broadly comprising a thickened cellulose wall which contains cytoplasm and a nucleus — the whole cellular organism looking, schematically, not unlike a kind of square-ish fried egg. The shrub outside my kitchen window comprises millions upon millions of these cells, each with its own unique shape and particular qualities, each getting on with the business of co-operative coexistence — and it is essential to the existence of the shrub that they all continue to do so. The continued functioning in its particular way of each group of cells is a necessary condition for the continued existence of this particular *Lavatera* 'Barnsley'.

Each cell and each aspect of each cell in turn comprises millions of atomic 'particles' — protons, neutrons and electrons — clustered in a particular way. The behaviour of each of these 'particles' is in turn conditioned by the qualities of the deeply mysterious sub-atomic environment within which they occur: gravity, the speed of light and other arcane factors each in turn conditioning the functioning of these atomic and sub-atomic events.

I hope we can now begin to see that the network of conditions which supports the existence of my *Lavatera* 'Barnsley' is infinite. Wherever one looks one sees another range of conditions and each of those conditions is in itself dependent upon another huge range of conditions. In every direction of time and space all we see are interrelated conditions. Looking at things in this way, we never arrive at any absolutely definitive 'essence', any fixed, final, unchanging essential nature.

All the phenomena of the world, without exception, arise in dependence upon conditions, and with the cessation of those conditions the phenomena which depend upon them also cease. Behind, above, beyond this vast network of conditions there exists nothing at all. The entire vast unfathomable cosmos is nothing but an ever changing network of related conditions, and wherever we look into it, if we look with a calm, concentrated and fearless gaze, we see infinite depths of inter-connectedness. Seeing in this way, with the unclouded eye of spiritual insight, is:

> To see a World in a grain of sand
> And a Heaven in a wild-flower,
> Hold Infinity in the palm of your hand
> And eternity in an hour.[5]

Another image for this same spiritual insight is that of Indra's Net:

Far away in the heavenly abode of the great god Indra, there is a wonderful net that has been hung by some cunning artificer in such a manner that it stretches out infinitely in all directions. In accordance with the extravagant taste of deities, the artificer has hung a single glittering jewel in each 'eye' of the net, and since the net is infinite in all dimensions, the jewels are infinite in number. There hang the jewels, glittering like stars of the first magnitude, a wonderful sight to behold. If we now arbitrarily select one of those jewels for inspection and look closely at it, we will discover that in its polished surface there are reflected all the other jewels in the net, infinite in number. Not only that, but each of the jewels reflected in this one jewel is also reflecting all the other jewels, so that there is an infinite reflecting process occurring.[6]

This is not, however, our normal mode of perception. We tend not to see things as they really are. Part of the reason for this is that we are beguiled by language.

Because we have a word or set of words to describe a phenomenon we tend to think that word or set of words points to an 'essence', something fixed and unchanging. I can speak of 'the *Lavatera* "Barnsley" outside my kitchen window' and this certainly identifies one particular current pattern of appearances, events, waves and particles, but we must beware of thinking that because we can speak in this way and point to something which effectively approximates to that description for the time being, we have thus actually identified anything which has an independent existence over and above the current nexus of conditions which support it. 'The map is not the area it represents.' Words are not the things they point to. Because we have a generally applicable label for certain patterns of phenomena does not mean that those phenomena exist independently of the conditions currently occurring. And, of course, the same applies to each and every one of those conditions themselves: just because we can speak of cells, or atoms, or waves and particles, or events in history, does not mean that in identifying them we have identified anything more 'real' than the plant they comprise. Each of these in turn depends upon other conditions. All existence, without exception, is entirely contingent.

When the conditions change, my *Lavatera* 'Barnsley' changes. It is in constant motion according to the seasons, according to the wind, sun and rain. It grows and decays, flowers in the summer, drops some of its leaves in the autumn and if the next occupant of this house doesn't like it will end up on the compost heap rotting. Although it makes sense in English to say 'it changes', there is, in reality, no 'it' to change, for when the *Lavatera* has become compost where is the 'it' which was the *Lavatera*?

The Buddhist principle of conditionality which I have outlined here points to the fact that all phenomena are ultimately devoid of 'essence'. They are, to use an important Buddhist concept, 'empty'. And the same is true of you and me: we have no fixed, final, identifiable self-hood. Everything that we call 'ourselves' is simply a changing pattern of inter-relationships — patterns which are inextricably part of the great flux of conditions.

> *No doer of the deeds is found,*
> *No one who ever reaps their fruit;*
> *Empty phenomena roll on:*
> *This view alone is right and true.*[7]

And yet we all cling, however unconsciously, to the idea that we have a 'self'; something which is 'us in our essential nature', something fixed and enduring, separate in its essentials from the rest of the universe.

This picture we have of ourselves is both false and limiting. Its principal limitation lies in its restriction of the possibility of change for the better. If we have a 'self', an essential nature which is fixed and enduring, then there is a limit to the extent to which we can grow as individuals. One hears examples of this idea all the time: 'I am who I am. I cannot change and you must accept me for what I am.' The idea that we were all somehow made to a particular pattern and set upon life's course by an unseen creator God runs deeply, albeit most often unconsciously, through contemporary Western society. We think we are who we are and there is a limit to the extent to which we can be expected to improve ourselves.

The Buddha's revolutionary insight, however, destroys this idea. The principle of conditionality makes it plain that we have no abiding essence. We are who we are solely in dependence upon all the myriad conditions which have preceded us. We become who we will become in dependence upon the conditions of the present and future. If we set about creating conditions which support change for the better then we will, inevitably, change for the better, and there is no limit to how much better we can become.

These ideas are unlike anything we have come to expect of religious discourse in the West. But then, the voice of Buddhism has only recently begun to join the conversation. As Buddhism begins to play more and more of a part on the Western cultural and religious scene, no doubt our received ideas of what religious discourse ought to be like will change accordingly. And Buddhism *is* beginning to emerge more from the darkness in which, so far as the West is concerned, it remained hidden for the last 2,500 years.

The Buddha's teachings have begun to diffuse quite widely into Western culture. The language of 'growth and development', for example, which is routinely used by psychotherapists and even corporate consultants, often includes significant elements of Buddhist thought. Doctors prescribe meditation as a treatment for stress; vegetarian food is widely available; environmentalists use Buddhist concepts; rap-singers rap on about 'Boodah'; and newspaper leader writers refer to Buddhist ideas and attitudes without feeling any need to explain themselves further.

One can never predict the future, but perhaps this is the start of a major cultural shift. For the history of Buddhism shows that whenever the teachings of the Buddha have entered a culture and begun to have an effect upon it, that culture eventually comes to be radically transformed by the encounter.

Today, more than half the world's population live in countries where Buddhism is now, or has been, dominant[8]. Siddhartha Gautama, the man who came to be the Buddha, was thus one of the most influential men who ever lived. Who was he?

Siddhartha Gautama was born about 485 years before the Christian era, in the borderlands of India and Nepal, near the foothills of the Himalayas. Growing up in an aristocratic family, he passed his early years in a life of ease and privilege. He had everything a young nobleman of his time might desire — a beautiful wife, a son, a social position — but he was not happy. For what was the meaning of it all? You're born, you experience some happiness, some sadness, you grow old, you get sick and you die. Is that all there is? Is that all?

That experience of the fundamental unsatisfactoriness of things is quite universal. Most people have it at some point in their lives. But most of us turn away from it and pretend it hasn't happened. Siddhartha, however, was a man of immense integrity. He couldn't simply brush his questions aside and get on with the business of statecraft, warriorship and family life. And so, at the age of twenty-nine, turning his back on family, comfort and social position, leaving behind all that his society valued, he set out into the wilderness, intent upon discovering the truth of things.

Indian religious life at this time was divided into two broad strands. There was the old religion of the *Vedas*, controlled by a priestly caste and associated with civil life and government, and there were the wandering mendicants — homeless ascetics living on the margins of civic life, subsisting on alms, intent upon spiritual liberation. Siddhartha became a wanderer.

It was commonly accepted at the time that one liberated the spirit by denying the body and Siddhartha took up the practice of religious austerity. For six years he strove for liberation by these means. Going naked, he reduced his food intake to next to nothing and endured horrifying privations. He sought out the renowned teachers of his time, became proficient in meditation and developed a great reputation for his ascetic determination. He soon attracted a following of his own and became renowned throughout northern India, but still he wasn't satisfied. Six years into his ascetic career he decided that privation wasn't going to lead him to the insights he sought and he began to eat in moderation. Disgusted with such backsliding, his followers abandoned him.

In this state of acute existential aloneness: without followers, friends or family, Siddhartha firmly renewed his resolution to seek out the truth and, sitting down under a tree on the evening of the full moon in May, he entered into meditation. Over the course of that night his meditation deepened and intensified. All the different energies of his being — physical, emotional, mental and spiritual - began to flow together in a single unified stream, growing ever stronger, brighter and more intense. He entered into states of consciousness never before experienced by any human being. Time and space ceased to delimit his consciousness. All the negative emotions, the many subtle manifestations of craving and aversion, fell away and the barriers between his own mind and that of others completely dissolved. Wherever he turned his attention he saw clearly into the true nature of things. All delusions were finally destroyed. He was free of all bonds. He realized that at last his quest was over. He had gained Enlightenment. Siddhartha Gautama had become the Buddha — the One Who Knows; the One Who is Awake.

The Buddha realized that although his realization was abstruse and difficult to comprehend — that it could only be obtained by dedicated striving and spiritual discipline — nonetheless there were many beings in the world who were willing and able to make that effort, and so he embarked on his long career as a spiritual teacher. Soon he had gathered about him a band of disciples who shared the experience of Enlightenment and he sent them off to wander in the world, living on alms, teaching the path to Enlightenment for the welfare of all.

For the next forty-five years the Buddha wandered through all of Northern India and wherever he went he taught. People in their thousands flocked to hear him teach. Kings, courtesans, traders, mendicants, householders — he attracted disciples from all walks of life and many of these came to share his spiritual realization.

Living as we do in a highly complex age, dependent on technological wizardry, buffered by possessions and awash in a
sea of media information, it is hard for us to imagine the
towering influence upon his time, and indeed upon all of
subsequent history, of this extraordinary man from the
margins of society. For the Buddha and his mendicant followers continued to live in the margins. They were at home in
the wilderness. Dressed in crude robes made by sewing up
discarded rags, with only a bowl for begging food and a few
simple implements, they led lives of stark simplicity, dedicated to spiritual striving. And yet their influence was
immense. By the time of the Asokan Empire, around 250BCE,
the Indian subcontinent was largely Buddhist and missionar-
ies were being sent westward to the Greek kingdoms in
Bactria and southward to Sri Lanka. Over the course of the
next millennium the Buddha's teachings had spread and
taken root in all of the countries of Asia.

The Buddha's teachings are known to Buddhists as the
Dharma — one of a small handful of terms which are best left
untranslated. It stands for all those doctrines and methods
which point out the way to spiritual liberation.

These teachings didn't begin to be written down until about
the first century BCE. Before that the facts of the Buddha's
life and the contents of his teaching were preserved in a
vast oral 'literature' — transmitted down the generations in
a prodigious enterprise of oral recitation. Having eventually
been written down, in Pali, Sanskrit or other variants of
Indian contemporary language, the traditional Buddhist
teachings developed and expanded. New material was
brought in and a vast canonical literature comprising
records of the Buddha's discourses and discussions, stories,
parables, poems and analyses gradually grew up. With the

passing of time, the tree of Buddhism has sprouted new branches and stems as great Enlightened masters brought their own particular insights to bear on it. Apart from its existence in literary form, there are also oral lineages of teaching transmission, from master to disciple, and even purely mental lineages, where the nature of reality is 'pointed out' in direct experience, unmediated by texts or liturgy. The teachings can be transmitted in any way that results in people being brought closer to an experience of ultimate truth.

Now Buddhism has come to the West. Indeed, the very term 'Buddhism' is of Western origin. Before the 19th century it had never been used at all and no equivalent to it existed in any of the languages of the East or the West. It only began to come into common usage around about the 1830s, when it was first used to describe some of the different kinds of religious belief that the early Victorians were beginning to come into contact with in their wanderings around Asia[9]. Over the next few decades, the word Buddhism was gradually distinguished from other new words (such as Hinduism) and eventually, by the 1860s, it came to be associated exclusively with those people who followed the teachings of the Buddha and practised a religion or a way of life they themselves called simply the Dharma — the Truth, the Path, or the Way Things Are.

The distinction between these two ideas, 'Buddhism' and 'the Dharma', is important. The Dharma, the teaching of the Buddha, is trans-cultural. It describes the way the world works, the way things really are, as well as all the different means by which ultimate reality can be apprehended. It is true for all times and in all places. 'Buddhism', on the other hand, is culture-relative. It is the product of the interaction between the Buddha's teachings, on the one hand, and on the other all the various cultures within which those teachings have been expressed. Whenever the teachings encountered a new cultural context and took root there, a new 'Buddhism' came into being. Thus we speak of Tibetan Buddhism, or Japanese Buddhism and so on.

As the teachings spread and interacted with the cultures in which they found themselves, they grew ever more complex and differentiated and today we are faced with a bewildering variety of Buddhist forms. There is Japanese Zen and Shin, Chinese Ch'an; Thai, Sri Lankan, Burmese, Laotian and Cambodian Theravada; Tibetan and Mongolian Vajrayana: a whole host of schools, sects and sub-sects which themselves are subdivisions of Tibetan Buddhism, Chinese Buddhism, Korean Buddhism and so on. At the heart of all of these different 'Buddhisms' there is one and the same Dharma, one and the same fundamental teaching. All the different Buddhisms, in their essentials, point to the same ultimate reality, and they are all, in their own ways, descriptions of the ways in which that reality can come to be apprehended by those individuals who make the effort to do so.

Today, in any major European, American or Antipodean city, one may encounter any number of different Buddhist centres. There are representatives of Japanese or Korean Zen; the main Nichiren Buddhist sects; the Chinese Ch'an, Pure Land and Tien Tai schools; the Tibetan Nyingmapa, Kagyupa, Sakyapa and Gelugpa schools; and various of the Sri Lankan, Thai and Burmese Theravadin *nikayas*, to name but a few.

In this vast maze of Buddhism it isn't always easy to see the essentials. And, fascinating though all these 'Buddhisms' may be, it is the Dharma — the teachings which lead to liberation — that people really need.

Newcomers to Buddhism are not in a position to distinguish what is essential, what are the teachings of the Buddha, from the cultural trappings and embellishments within which they are couched. When someone living in the West goes along to a Buddhist centre, it is not usually because they want to know more about Tibetan culture, or because they want to know about how people lead their religious life in Thailand. Most Westerners who look to Buddhism do so because they are in search of the truth. They want to know what is really going on, with themselves and others, and they want some guidance as to how they might live. They are looking for the Dharma, not just another variant on Buddhism. They want to learn how to change themselves for the better, not how one bows in the Japanese tradition, or what Sri Lankans think is the most appropriate way to address a monk.

The truths which the Buddha taught, however, require a vehicle for expression. No idea or concept can stand alone in pristine isolation, somehow separated from the language within which it is expressed. Every communication takes place within a context. The Buddha's teachings therefore require a context within which they can be communicated and within which they can be practised. The Dharma therefore needs Buddhism and Westerners who seek the teachings need to find Buddhist forms where the 'Buddhism' least obscures these — where what is merely cultural and therefore peripheral can be clearly distinguished from what is essential. Just as the encounter between the Buddha's teachings and Tibetan culture produced the various forms of Tibetan Buddhism, and the encounter between the teachings and Chinese culture produced the various forms of Chinese Buddhism, so in the West today we find a nascent Western Buddhism: the Wheel of the Dharma is turning yet another round.

Buddhism, with its psychological acuity, clarity of expression, profound symbolic imagery, transformative methodologies and transcendental insight has now encountered the most technologically advanced culture that there has ever been.

Never before in the history of Buddhism's journey around the world has any people had the kind of access to all the varieties of Buddhist history and culture that we in the West have today. Modern communications media and the relative ease of global travel have substantially diminished the gulf between the East and the West. Eastern teachers migrate West to give teachings, Western students fly East for conferences, retreats and meetings with teachers. There are Buddhist centres and retreat centres in all the major population centres in the United States and Europe.

Buddhist canonical literature is vast. In its most developed form, the Tibetan *Kanjur*, it effectively comprises a small library. Although not all of this has yet been translated and published, we can nonetheless be reasonably certain that by now we have translations available of all the major works of Buddhist literature from all the traditions. Not since the destruction of the great monastic universities in India in medieval times have so many variants on the tradition been available at any one time (and since then even more variants have emerged).

The Western art of historical analysis, together with the tools of 'higher criticism' which contemporary Buddhologists inherit from theology, combined with the sheer volume of data available to them, give the Buddhists of today a unique perspective on the broad range of the Buddhist tradition.

Almost every day, a new Buddhist publication sees the light of day — a new translation, a new commentary, a new critique.

We in the West today stand as heirs to the entire Buddhist tradition, we have more variants of it available to us than have any previous people anywhere. In these circumstances, with the whole of Buddhism available to us, if we want to practise the teachings we don't have to pick and choose from between the different schools and traditions and identify solely with that particular manifestation of Buddhism — say Theravada Buddhism, or Tibetan Karma Kagyu Buddhism, or Korean Zen Buddhism.

Nor do we have to abandon our own rich cultural tradition and blindly adopt Asian customs and practices. Westerners who wish to practise Buddhism are able to examine the whole broad range of the Buddhist tradition and draw from it whatever they find useful, whatever its native provenance. In this task one needs a guide, a teacher or spiritual friend who has more experience of the path than one has oneself, for the tradition is vast and can be bewildering. But one must beware of the guide who claims that his or her form of Buddhism is the best and highest path, for such statements always only indicate an ignorance of the tradition as a whole.

Only by taking the teachings to heart, by putting them into practice in daily life, can we ever come to glimpse their true meaning for ourselves. The future of Western Buddhism is not to be found in the scholarly academies, helpful though their products are to the sincere practitioner. Rather it is to be found wherever men and women come together to learn the teachings and to put them into practice.

For the teachings cannot exist only in the abstract. The Buddha was not akin to a modern philosopher. He did not teach a set of theories which, perhaps because of the elegance of their conceptual relationships, can be thought somehow to have value in and of themselves. The Buddha taught in order to end the suffering of living beings. If a teaching doesn't conduce to the ending of suffering, he once said, then it is not his teaching. The Dharma, the teachings, therefore have to be practised, and the people who practise the teachings are known as the Sangha — the spiritual community. In its broadest usage, the term 'Sangha' (which is another of those words which I will occasionally leave untranslated) refers to all those men and women, throughout time, who have taken the Buddha's teachings to heart and put them into practice in their daily lives, and just as Buddhism needs the Dharma, so too it needs the Sangha. For the teachings are not transmitted in records alone. They are largely transmitted through relationships between people. Practitioners with more experience of the teachings pass them on to those with less experience. Thus, for the last 2,500 years, the Buddha's teachings have been transmitted down a vast network of relationships between more and less experienced Buddhists.

The Buddha; the Dharma, his teachings; and the Sangha, the spiritual community — between them make up the Three Jewels, the three highest ideals of Buddhism. Now they have come to the West.

As Western Buddhism comes into being it is essential that Western Buddhists stay true to the essence of the Buddhist tradition. At the same time they cannot be bound exclusively to past formulations of the teachings. For the teachings themselves are not finally contained in any of their previous formulations. All the many methods, doctrines and formulas are only a means — fingers pointing to the moon — and one must not mistake the finger of the teaching for the moon of spiritual realization. Through the practice of ethics, meditation, study and reflection, however, Western Buddhists can begin to make the teachings their own and to express them in terms which are appropriate to our time and place.

In approaching Buddhism, however, we must be conscious of our backgrounds. Western culture is deeply conditioned by its Judaeo-Christian and rationalist antecedents. We cannot simply superimpose the structures of Buddhism on non-Buddhist foundations and hope that they will stand. One of the first tasks faced by the emerging Western Buddhism is therefore a rigorous questioning of its own assumptions — to what extent are they truly Buddhist? To what extent Christian, post-Christian, Rousseauist, Marxist, feminist or rationalist? In taking up the practice of Buddhism one must be prepared to leave the baggage of one's conditioned presuppositions behind and think things out anew.

Nor need Westerners be in too much of a hurry to forge a single, coherent, Western Buddhist doctrine. Although the fundamental principles of Buddhism retain a high degree of coherence throughout the many Buddhist schools and traditions, subtle differences of doctrinal interpretation abound. At this stage in the emergence of Western Buddhism we are under no obligation to hoist our colours upon any of these different masts. With the tools of higher criticism and with our unique historical perspective we can begin to see how different doctrines emerged in relation to prevailing conditions.

Taking a longer view backwards than any Buddhists have ever been able to before, we can see, for example, an emerging dialectical pattern, as Buddhists down the ages have engaged in a successive process of subtly affirming or negating the ultimate constituents of reality. As I shall show, such positions are in the nature of thought and language — when dealing with ultimate truths human beings can do no other than to adopt a subtly affirmative or subtly negative standpoint. But modern Western Buddhists have no need to *finally* adhere to any one of these antecedent positions. Sometimes we may choose to use affirmative language, sometimes negative. 'Doctrine is doctrine for the sake of method'. The aim of Buddhist thought is not to hammer out a single consistent theory — it is the liberation of living beings by whatever methods serve.

Modern Western culture is marked by an unprecedented degree of technological sophistication and material abundance. It is highly complex, egalitarian (at least in theory) and deeply fragmented. It has given rise to some of the world's most sublime cultural creations and some of its most horrifying atrocities. How will Buddhism impact on a society like this? What distinguishes Western Buddhism from all the 'Buddhisms' which have preceded it? As the third generation of Western Buddhist teacher begins to emerge in the West, what are they teaching?

---

1. *Majjhima-Nikaya* II.32, trans. I. B. Horner in *Middle Length Sayings*, Vol. II, Pali Text Society, 1975, p. 229.

2. Dr. Nalinaksha Dutt, *Aspects of Mahayana Buddhism and its Relation to Hinayana*, Luzac, 1930, p.51, gives nine canonical references for this composite 'quotation', from Pali and Sanskrit sources.

3. *paticca-samuppada, pratitya-samutpada.*

4. Pali *dhamma*, Sanskrit *dharma.*

5. 'Auguries of Innocence', in *Blake: Complete Writings*, ed. G. Keynes, Oxford, 1966.

6. Francis H. Cook, *Hua-yen Buddhism: The Jewel Net of Indra*, Pennsylvania State University Press, 1977. The simile of Indra's Net occurs in the *Avatamsaka Sutra*, a text which had an enormous impact on Chinese Buddhism. Indra is not a Buddhist figure, but the Buddhist tradition never hesitated to incorporate elements of local mythology for didactic purposes.

7. *Path of Purification*, Ch. XIX. Trans. Nanamoli Thera, Bst. Publication Society, Kandy, 1979.

8. Joanne O'Brien and Martin Palmer, *The State of Religion Atlas*, Touchstone, 1993.

9. Phillip C. Almond, *The British Discovery of Buddhism*, Cambridge University Press, 1988.

Chapter 2

The Nature of Existence

The picture of the web of conditions shows, in a two-dimensional model, how everything arises solely in dependence upon conditions and how all things are interrelated. What it does not show is how we ourselves fit into the picture – how did we come to be as we are and what can we do about it?

I remember when I first began to practise Buddhism, I used from time to time to badger my kind and patient teacher — 'How does it all work?' I wanted to know, 'how did things come to be like this? Like this, of all things.' For it seemed to me that the world we all live in was somehow absurd. Why did it turn out quite like this? How come our bodies are as they are? How come we have to eat to survive? How come we crave sex so much? And why is an orange like an orange? Or a spider like a spider? The universe is all so intricate, so multifarious, so strange...

The Buddha never bothered to try to answer questions like this. He realized that any attempt to do so simply propelled one into an infinite regress — there was always another question that could be asked. No answer would ever be final.

Some ways of questioning are fruitless. There is, however, much more that *can* usefully be said about the way the world works. In particular, if we can get some idea of the emotional underpinning which supports our tendency to see things in too fixed a way, then we will be in a better position to begin to work to change ourselves, to bring our view of ourselves and the world more into accordance with how things really are. The more clearly we see how things really are, the more we behave in accordance with that insight, the less suffering our behaviour will produce — for ourselves and others.

The picture of the web of conditions shows how things are interrelated. A more dynamic model, mobile and three-dimensional, which takes our own emotional predispositions into account, might help us to see how we have become who we are and how we can begin to exercise choice and go beyond our current limitations.

The Sea of Conditions is vast — infinitely deep: unbounded in all directions. It contains nothing less than the past and present of the entire universe. All 'matter' is contained in it — all cells, chemicals, particles and waves. It contains all of human history: all information, all ideas. All these ideas, cells, chemicals, and bits of information are themselves constantly changing and rearranging as they flow together in an infinitely vast array of different patterns.

Looking over the surface of the ocean, we can see some of these patterns. Here the sea is smooth and calm, there it is rippled, in another place it foams and bubbles. Here it is choppy, there we see waves. In one section of the sea there are a large number of whirlpools — vortices of different sizes and different shapes. Each vortex is unique, each has its own characteristics. Some are larger than others, some are deeper than others, some are vigorous, some are languid. They come into being, subsist for a time, and then disappear as the sea flows and changes in constant motion.

Each vortex represents an individual human life. We come into being and take shape from the conditions available to us. The cells, chemicals, biological matter and all the other

conditions of our lives give shape to our being. Different frag-
ments of the ideas of Marx, Christ, Thoreau, the Beatles,
Rousseau, Walt Whitman, Raymond Chandler, Freud, Picasso,
Adam Smith, Jefferson, Keats, Einstein, the advertising industry, Shakespeare, Rembrandt, Henry Ford, Chaucer, Ian
Fleming, and the Buddha drift in this Sea of Conditions. They
flow into our vortex, give it shape, flow down and flow out.
The history of our parents and our culture flows in, flows down
and flows out. All our inherited ideas of good and bad; all the
cells which replicate and die in our bodies; all the viruses
which affect our health; all the colours, shapes, sounds, smells,
tastes and ideas we ever experience, flow in, flow down and
flow out. All our memories, sensations, emotions, desires and
actions flow in to the vortex, shape it and flow out.

In reality we are not ultimately separate from the rest of the
Sea of Conditions, from all the vast immensity of life itself. But
we don't see it like that. 'Human kind cannot bear very much
reality''. In order to get by from day to day, in order to get on
with the apparently urgent business of survival, we narrow the
scope of our vision to more manageable proportions.

Grabbing onto some conditions as they drift by, pushing away
others, we each create an apparently workable ego-identity
for ourselves and then spend the rest of our lives in a desperate attempt to preserve that identity.

Everything that lives is subject to decay. All conditioned things
are impermanent. To be alive is to change. Without change we
would be absolutely inert. But the un-Enlightened human
condition is to fight change every inch of the way.

We are human and alive because we fight for existence. At any
moment the Sea of Conditions throws up potential threats to
our continued existence. Walking down any urban street, cars

hurl past us at life-threatening speeds, sometimes only inches from where we walk. A single slip, a single misjudgement and we would be dead. If our temperature dropped just a few degrees for too long, we'd die of hypothermia; if it rose too high for too long, we'd die of heat exhaustion. We avoid poisonous food and bacteria, viruses and any number of life-threatening situations quite instinctively and unconsciously. The fact that we are now alive shows how skilled we are in avoiding death; how tenaciously, how desperately we cling to existence.

Bound up with this strong urge for survival is a deep desire for identity — to be fixed, to be separate, *to be real*. In conse- quence, we cling to one part of the vortex only. We identify ourselves exclusively with one small aspect of our experience and try to block out all the rest. We try to keep our self- consciousness pinned down at a low part of the vortex, where it cycles around a narrow point. We don't see the clear sky above or the surface of the vast sea all around. We pin ourselves down at a point where we think we can cope with what surrounds us and we call that point 'me'. That, we think, is what we really are; that is what we have to protect; that is what must survive. And survive we do — but at a cost. Ordinary human life is marked by quite high levels of anguish and anxiety.

Modern psychoanalysis traces all neurosis, including the low- grade neurosis we call normality, back to anxiety.[2]

Towards the beginning of the twentieth century Sigmund Freud revolutionized psychological thinking when he suggested that repression was the key to the understanding of human anxiety. When a thought, feeling, memory or other mental occurrence makes us uncomfortable and we don't want to deal with it consciously, we may choose to ignore or 'forget' it. We can then get on with what we want to — but at a price. Part of our mental energy must be spent resisting what has been repressed, keeping it out of consciousness; so we experience persistent tension. Or, even worse, what has been repressed may return to consciousness in a distorted form as a symptom of neurosis or even psychosis, these symptoms being seen as symbolic representations of the repressed material.

The younger Freud, treating middle-class Viennese patients for hysteria and phobia, concluded that sexual repression was our primary repression. This is understandable, given the circumstances in which he found himself, but as he got older his attention naturally shifted from sex to death and he broadened the scope of his enquiry to include issues such as the repression of the fact of death.

Buddhism goes one stage further. What we are really repressing, underneath everything else — at the very root — is the fact of our ultimate non-existence. More than anything else, we want simply *to be*, and all the anguish and suffering of our lives comes down to this fundamentally frustrated desire, a desire which can only be fulfilled by becoming truly real. We can only become truly real when we are able to live out of a sense of the true nature of our existence. For our existence is entirely contingent. There is nothing fixed, final and enduring about ourselves and the world we inhabit. Such existence as we have is only ever relative but we desperately want it to be absolute.

But none of the strategies which we implement in the face of our desire for permanence have the desired outcome. Our fundamental problem is that although we want to become truly 'real', we can only achieve this by letting go of what is 'false': that is by letting go of our limited, ego-delineated sense of ourselves — and that is not easy. The truth of conditionality points to the entirely contingent and provisional nature of our 'ordinary' view of ourselves. Like everything else, we are constantly changing. There is nothing we can identify as finally, ultimately, 'what we really are' — in our essential nature. Our essential nature is 'no nature'. In reality we are not fixed, unchanging, separate selves but rather we are a part of the ever changing flow of life — the flux of the Sea of Conditions. The only way to become 'truly real' is by letting go of our fixed, ego-delineated view of ourselves. Only by giving up our attachment to the illusion that there is a real, final and definitive boundary between ourselves and everything else can we ever become truly real.

According to Buddhism, we keep our consciousness pinned down at the bottom of the vortex by way of three fundamentally conditioning impulses — craving, aversion and delusion, reflexes of our relentless desire for continued existence.

Craving is the mechanism by which we try to augment and secure our ego-identity by including in it things from 'outside' of it. By grasping onto things we like, things which give us pleasure, things with which we wish to be associated, or be seen to be associated with, we constantly strive to build up a firm ego-identity.

Pleasure, power and status are qualities with which we all wish to be associated, and, although we may derive these from very different things and experience them in different ways, we are all united in our delusive quest to build our identities on these infirm foundations.

We use them to fill that empty feeling inside which is simply part of the ordinary, un-Enlightened human condition. Whenever we encounter this sense of inner emptiness we try to assuage it with something: anything. To this end we use chocolate bars, beer, mindless television watching, compulsive shopping, sex, stamp-collecting, train spotting, gambling, over-work, mindless chatter and even compulsive altruism: anything to plug the gap, to give us a sense of 'being real', a sense of being present. This low-level sense of anxiety and inner emptiness is one of the main levers with which the Western advertising industry manipulates us so adroitly. It is the motive force behind consumerism.

Aversion is the mechanism by which we try to secure our ego-identity by rejecting any form of connection between it and the object we despise. Whether we feel aversion for our boss, our neighbour, aubergines, city life, or people of another race, religion or sexual preference, the fundamental mechanism is the same — we are fixing ourselves and seeking to preserve our experience within the boundaries of the known and famil-iar. We define ourselves as much by what we reject as we do by what we accept. All the horrors of sectarian violence which this decade has witnessed come down in the end to the futile attempts of groups of people to establish secure ego-identities bounded by race, religion or cultural history.

Delusion is the endlessly beguiling notion that our ego-identities can in fact be preserved. It is the underlying unconscious belief which we all share that we can keep the universal tides of impermanence at bay with the futile bulwarks which are erected by the forces of craving and aversion. Everything always changes. *We* always change. Nothing we can do can ever keep change at bay and yet, deludedly, we scamper about forever seeking to recreate a fixed and stable sense of ourselves.

This is the human condition. We experience some pleasure and some pain. The force of craving compels us always to attempt to incorporate into ourselves whatever we can of pleasurable experience. Aversion compels us to eject what we see as painful, and, oscillating between these twin poles of experience, we hold ourselves within a narrow band of experience, painfully confined within the narrow segment of possible experience which we call 'ourselves', delusively unaware of the vast potentiality of being which is the Sea of Conditions — the entire cosmos.

Buddhism, however, asserts that this is not the only way we can be. We can begin to undo the bonds of craving, aversion and delusion. In doing so, to extend our analogy, we'll begin to rise up within the vortex and we'll see more of what surrounds us. By becoming more open to new modes of experience, new ways of being, we can begin to drop our narrow, delusive self-preoccupation, and consequent self-limitation. Instead we can develop new, more expansive modes of consciousness with greater awareness of the rest of reality and more empathy with the rest of life. Rising up the vortex we can begin to identify more with life itself, less with our own narrow segment of it.

Such an identification, however, is not merely an intellectual matter. It is not enough simply to agree with the different ideas, images or formulations of Buddhism on an intellectual level alone, although most of us necessarily begin at this level. It is one thing to agree with things intellectually but it is quite another to consistently behave as if they were true. In between these two positions lies the whole of the Buddhist spiritual path.

Buddhists are those people who accept the truth of the Buddha's teaching on conditionality, and who consequently seek to apply to their daily lives methods of personal development which have this truth as their basis and which in turn lead towards an ever deeper realisation of it.

One of the most basic statements of methodology in traditional Buddhism is embodied in the formula of the Four Noble Truths:

1. We experience life as intrinsically unsatisfying.

We have a ceaseless itch to 'get what we need', to 'put things right'. Caught up in a narrow, ego-delineated level of experience we constantly bump up against the unsatisfactory nature of our own confinement. Because nothing lasts, and yet we always want pleasure to continue indefinitely, we are bound to experience frustration.

2. The cause of this kind of experience is craving (and its complement, aversion).

So long as we are involved in this desperate process of grabbing for some things and pushing others away we will continue to experience the world as limited and painful.

3. Through the cessation of craving, unsatisfactoriness too ceases.

If we can let go of this tendency to grab or push away, then the conditions which create our sense of dissatisfaction will no longer arise.

4. There is a path leading away from suffering.

There are ways in which we can do this. The Buddhist path enables one to change even these fundamental orientations.

We have no essence. Who we are is not somehow 'given'. We weren't made to a fixed, pre-determined pattern. We are more fluid than that, constantly changing in response to prevailing conditions. By beginning to take control of some of the conditions of our lives we can begin to 'make' ourselves more consciously.

Buddhists sometimes speak of this lack of essence as 'emptiness', or 'voidness'. In the quasi-Buddhist psychedelic circles

I used to move in during the early 1970s we used to talk of 'The Void', as if the lack of essence were somehow an embodied thing, having an independent existence somewhere. I used to imagine it as a kind of vast whirlpool of black nothingness, spinning out in psychic space, and I believed that all the psychedelic adventurer had to do was somehow to find 'The Void' and hurl himself in — then you'd be enlightened and everything would be OK.

Of course it's not quite like that (although my enchantment with the idea did at least keep me out other kinds of trouble). Emptiness, or voidness, isn't a thing. It doesn't exist somewhere else. Rather, it is right here and everywhere. It is the real nature of all things. But the term 'emptiness' can be confusing. For some people, perhaps, it has too nihilistic an association. It might be more useful to use a term coined by Herbert Guenther: rather than emptiness, we can speak of 'the open dimension of being'. Because all phenomena, including ourselves, are devoid of essence, nothing is ever fixed and final. Everything always changes. In other words, there is an open, unpredictable dimension to every event. As we shall see, the practical consequences of this fact are immense. It implies that everything can be changed for the better.

As we live our lives from day to day, we don't usually take the 'open dimension' into account. We tend to think that things are as they are and will always continue to be so — they are going to keep running along the known, predictable ruts they have always run along. We derive a sense of security from this sense of pseudo-predictability, and we work hard to keep it in place. Although things may be a little boring at times, and we may be a little anxious, at least we seem to be fairly safe.

This view of things is fundamentally delusive. Nothing is ever finally predictable and we are never really safe. Anything can happen at any time. The unknown constantly breaks through into the known. From moment to moment, we can never be sure what is going to happen next. Just when we think everything is safely buttoned down an unpredicted event occurs and we have to rearrange our view of things yet again.

We can take two different approaches to this inescapable fact of life. We can try to fight the unpredictability of things and anxiously try to keep everything tied down, or we can take a more creative approach.

Because things are intrinsically unstable everything can be changed. If they can be changed, they can be made better. In any situation it is therefore possible to move from 'less' to 'more'.

The move from less to more is the fundamental creative act. When we make something worthwhile which had not been before, we move from less to more. We can only do this by stepping outside of our rut, turning away from the predictable, the known, and entering the unknown: the open dimension.

This is the nature of every act of creation. Whether we make a picture or a poem; an omelette or a chair — we can do it with a staid, uncreative predictability or we can bring something fresh and vital to it. We can only do that by leaving the known behind and by having the confidence to step out into the open dimension.

Creativity in this sense isn't confined to making objects. We can turn towards the open dimension in every aspect of our lives. As we shall see, Buddhism judges the quality of our actions in dependence upon the mental state which gave rise to them. Creative actions arise from creative mental states. Creative mental states are those which are not primarily concerned in protecting a confined ego-identity by keeping everything running in safe and predictable ruts.

Struggling to preserve predictability, we just go on producing the same thing, again and again: trudging the same dreary round, repeating the same conversations, reading the same literature, watching the same TV, experiencing the same limited range of mental and emotional states. Creativity comes from turning towards the open dimension, accepting the ultimately unknowable nature of things, and thereby being free to move from less to more.

The Buddhist spiritual path is the constant attempt to move from less to more in every aspect of our lives. It comprises all those doctrines and methods which Buddhists down the ages have successfully used to foster and sustain creative mental states.

So long as we believe we have a fixed self and act as if we do, we will experience the continual friction produced by the dissonance between what we believe, how we behave, and how things really are. Reality, rubbing up against our illusions, generates suffering — for ourselves and for others.

And yet we can do no other. Unenlightened, we pass our days in fields of attachment, driven by subtler or grosser forms of craving and aversion, delusively questing for security within the intrinsically insecure. Phenomena constantly present themselves to us with an alluring seductiveness, holding out the vain hope of true being and lasting security. In the mental realm, the seductive character of mundane phenomena can be seen to manifest as a battleground of conflicting ideologies competing for our allegiance.[3]

Ideologies are seductive because in organising the world — our ideas and impressions — in a particular way, they give us a sense of the meaning of things and a sense of what our place in that structure of meaning is. The vast majority of ideologies support the delusion that we have a fixed and separate self.

Broadly speaking, there are two different kinds of ideology. Most common are those which seek to entrap. Once you are committed to them, they manifest conceptual devices to keep you within them. A Marxist who starts to doubt the validity of historical materialism might be told by his comrades to purge himself of his bourgeois tendencies. A fundamentalist Christian might be told that his doubts are from the devil and he must put them behind him and simply *believe*.

Then there are ideologies which seek to liberate. Such ideologies are designed to transcend themselves and be self-negating: to free us, ultimately, from dependence on all ideologies including their own. Buddhism, at its best, is a preeminent example of this. Buddhism itself is something to be ultimately transcended and left behind.

This idea is illustrated by the Parable of the Raft[4], in which the Buddha describes the predicament of a man on a journey who encounters a large stretch of water blocking his way. The traveller proceeds to gather sticks and grass together and builds himself a raft with which to cross over to the other side. When he has successfully done this, however, the Buddha asks his audience:

'I, depending on this raft, and striving with my hands and feet, crossed over safely to the beyond. Suppose now that I, having put this raft on my head, or having lifted it on my shoulder, should proceed as I desire?' What do you think about this, monks? If that

man does this, is he doing what should be done with that raft?

'No, Lord'.

What should that man do, monks, in order to do what should be done with that raft? In this case, monks, it might occur to that man who has crossed over, gone beyond: 'Now, this raft has been very useful to me. Depending on this raft and striving with my hands and feet, I have crossed over safely to the beyond. Suppose that I, having beached this raft on dry ground or having submerged it under the water, should proceed as I desire?' In doing this, monks, that man would be doing what should be done with that raft. Even so, monks, is the Parable of the Raft dhamma taught by me for crossing over, not for retaining.

Rafts are ultimately to be left behind. But this does not mean that we don't need a raft to cross to the further shore. We cannot simply dispense with all ideologies at will. To do so (imagining such an impossibility for a moment) would be to propel us into a state of mental chaos and confusion. *That* is not the 'further shore' which Buddhism speaks of.

But if a raft is something to be merely left behind, if language, ideas, concepts and thoughts are all ultimately to be transcended, what is their status here and now? If they are all *equally* non-transcendent, how then can we distinguish between them and how can we make any use of them? Are they not all equally flawed, all of them merely provisional? Buddhism addresses this question by distinguishing two different categories of truth. Ultimate Truth[5] and Conventional Truth[6].

Ultimate Truth is ineffable. Every predicate by which we

seek to define it will ultimately contradict our attempted definition. The structure of language and conceptualization is
such that we can only affirm something in relation to an
implied negation and negate something in relation to an
implied affirmation. By whatever means we seek to describe
a state which transcends the distinction between subject and
object, being and non-being, affirmation and negation, we
can, conceptually, only take our stand in one or another of
the above polarities. The structure of language and conceptualization ultimately allows of no other position and thus
Ultimate Truth is ultimately inexpressible.

Ultimate Truth is beyond dualistic understanding and beyond
dualistic expression. It is 'transcendental'. That the transcendental is inexpressible, however, does not mean that it is unat-
tainable, although it cannot be 'attained' by a limited ego-identity, as if it were merely another attribute that the limited
ego-identity could add onto itself. Rather, it involves the
complete abandonment of ego-identity. Thus, to demonstrate
the paradoxical nature of discussions of this kind, we can strive
to gain Enlightenment, but 'we' can never be Enlightened.

Enlightenment, Buddhahood, Nirvana — all are expressions
which point to the transcendental dimension. They are all, to
use a popular Zen Buddhist expression, 'Fingers pointing to
the Moon', and we must never mistake the finger for the
moon. The expression does not exhaustively define the state
expressed. So far as *we* are concerned, the transcendental is
'over the horizon' and there is nothing we can ultimately say
of it. But this does not mean that there is no path leading
towards the horizon, nor does it mean that we cannot see a
strong glow at the horizon and that we cannot see highly
significant signs and images which, although apparently on
this side of the horizon, nonetheless indicate that there is

something very significant taking place beyond our current field of vision.

Ultimate Truth is over the horizon. This side of the horizon we only have Conventional Truth. But that word 'only' doesn't signify a low level of value, for Conventional Truth includes the whole range of doctrines and methods which point to the horizon. That I am writing this at a computer in a cottage in Norfolk, England, is a statement of Conventional Truth. It may not describe the Ultimate Truth of what I am, but it does make it plain that I'm not now in London. Conventional truths are 'operative concepts'. They work. They provide an adequate description. If we act upon them, the outcomes are consistent with our expectations. Conventional Truth thus includes all the doctrines and formulae of Buddhism: whatever genuinely conduces towards Enlightenment. Conventional Truth is therefore the raft by which we reach the further shore, it is indispensable to anyone seeking the goal of Enlightenment. Although 'only' relatively true, its value is beyond price.

We are currently deluded. We are not Enlightened. The Buddhist path begins with the recognition of this fact. We may be able to range towards the horizon with our intellect: by considering the doctrinal formulations of Buddhism we get some limited idea of what it is that lies over the horizon. Moving toward the horizon with our imagination, we envisage images of Enlightenment, such as the Buddha and Bodhisattva figures depicted in Buddhist art. Ranging towards the horizon with our emotions, we engage in acts of devotion towards the magnificent prospects which our imagination reveals at the further reaches of the path. But essentially we live and act very much on this side of the horizon. We live as if the world were made up of ultimately discrete subjects and objects. Our actions are mainly governed by the motivations of appropriation and rejection. We constantly strive for recognition and affection. We act as if the things we possess, or wish we possessed, could give us lasting happiness and security. We are angry and disappointed when we don't get what we want, and we grieve when we lose what we thought we had. In short, we cling, however subtly, to views which stand in direct contradiction to the principles of Buddhism as expressed within Conventional Truth.

But, un-Enlightened, we cannot live without an ideology. Indeed, we are, in a sense, made up of nothing but competing ideologies. It is therefore very important to become conscious of the ideologies we hold and to replace Wrong Views (the ideologies which keep us entrapped) with Right Views (the ideologies which liberate).

Our views, however unconsciously we hold them, determine our actions. As we believe, so we do; as we do, so we become.

Unskilful mental states are preceded by mind, led by mind, and made up of mind. If one speaks or acts with an impure mind suffering follows him even as the cartwheel follows the hoof of the ox.

Skilful mental states are preceded by mind, led by mind, and made up of mind. If one speaks or acts with a pure mind happiness follows him like his shadow.[7]

One of the most concise and fundamental expressions of Right View in the Buddhist tradition is the teaching of the Three Characteristics of all Phenomena.[8]

All Conditioned things are impermanent. When with understanding one sees this, one becomes weary of suffering. This is the Way to Purity.

All Conditioned things are painful. When with understanding one sees this, one becomes weary of suffering. This is the Way to Purity.

All things whatsoever are devoid of unchanging selfhood. When with understanding one sees this, one becomes weary of suffering. This is the Way to Purity.[9]

All conditioned things are impermanent, unsatisfactory and insubstantial. To see things like this is to see them as they really are.

The principle of conditionality shows the impermanent and insubstantial nature of all phenomena. A consequence of this is that they cannot, of themselves, provide us with any lasting satisfaction. And yet we constantly treat the world as if it were permanent, substantial and ultimately satisfying. Thus deluded, we are wedded to a nexus of suffering. Not recognizing the impermanent and insubstantial nature of phenomena, we cycle between the twin poles of attraction and repulsion: endlessly unsatisfied, grabbing onto this, pushing away from that. And so it will go until we replace Wrong View with Right View, until we cease to behave as if phenomena are permanent, substantial and satisfying and start of behave as they are impermanent, insubstantial and incapable of providing ultimate satisfaction.

In other words, we need to treat the Conditioned as the Conditioned.

The goal of the Buddhist spiritual life is not the merging of oneself with an unchanging, all-embracing, Unconditioned Absolute — however that may be characterized. Rather, its objective is complete insight into the true nature of the Conditioned itself. To borrow an expression from Krishnamurti:

The unconditional acceptance of the Conditioned is the Unconditioned.

In our modern, 'heady' culture we cannot over-stress the fact that such an insight is not merely an intellectual matter, although the path to it may well begin with intellectual understanding.

'Insight', as we have seen, refers to a process of complete re-orientation — a complete rearrangement of all our faculties of thinking, perceiving and feeling such that we are irrevocably changed: so that our whole being accords more fully with the way things really are. Such an insight amounts to nothing less than complete liberation from all suffering and delusion. For when one sees that one has no fixed, separate self to protect and enhance; when one is beyond the grip of the forces of appropriation and rejection; when one identifies not with one's own life exclusively, but with all of life; then one dwells in a state of supreme equanimity and complete, spontaneous creativity, freely able to respond to circumstances as they arise with complete appropriateness. Seeing things as they really are, one acts always accordingly. This, in Buddhist terms, is the fullness of Wisdom and Compassion. And it is a goal to be approached in practice, not merely in theory.

Central to that practice, is the Buddhist idea of karma — the teaching that actions always have consequences.

---

1. T.S. Eliot, 'Burnt Norton', in *Four Quartets, Collected Poems*, Faber & Faber, London, 1963.

2. I am indebted for this analysis to David Loy — see his 'Buddhism and

Money', published in *Radical Conservatism: Buddhism in the Contemporary World*, I.N.E.B., Bangkok, 1990.

3. Again, I acknowledge my indebtedness to David Loy — ibid, footnote 2.

4. *Majjhima-Nikaya* I.135, trans. I. B. Horner in *Middle Length Sayings*, Vol I, Pali Text Society, 1967, p173.

5. *paramattha-sacca, paramartha-satya.*

6. *sammuti-sacca, samvrti-satya.*

7. *Dhammapada* verses 1 & 2, translated by Sangharakshita, unpublished.

8. *ti-lakkhana, tri-lakshana.*

9. *Dhammapada* 273-9.

Chapter 3

Karma, Consciousness and Creativity

> *Instant Karma's gonna get you*
> *Gonna knock you right on the head*
> *You better get yourself together*
> *Pretty soon you're gonna be dead*

John Lennon sang it like that; Boy George and the Culture Club took another approach:

> *Karma, Karma, Karma, Karma, Karma Chameleon,*
> *You come and go, you come and go...*

The word 'karma' has entered the English language. But in common usage the Buddhist and the Hindu ideas of karma tend to be conflated. Collins English Dictionary, for example, translates it as:

1. (Hinduism, Buddhism) The principle of retributive justice determining a person's state of life and the state of his reincarnations as the effect of his past deeds.

2. (Theosophy) The doctrine of inevitable consequence.

3. Destiny or fate.

The idea of divine, retributive justice is, of course, deeply rooted in our culture. As a young child I sometimes used to go to a kind of Saturday School at our local synagogue. There, amongst many other things, I learned that there was a huge book in Heaven and there was an angel whose specific job it was to write up in that book all the good and bad things that I got up to and that one day, when I died, all those things would be weighed up. More good than bad, I'd be OK. More bad than good — real trouble.

I don't think I ever explicitly believed it, but somewhere these ideas stick. The idea of divine retribution is part of the air we breathe in Judaeo-Christian cultures. The Buddhist approach to karma, however, has nothing at all to do with the idea of retribution — divine, cosmic or otherwise.

Karma literally means 'action' and, when used in a Buddhist context, it refers to those voluntary acts of body, speech and mind which make us what we are. Actions have consequences. Within the vast network of conditions which make up ourselves and the whole universe, changes in any dimension ripple outwards generating further effects. But the way in which conditions interact is not simply random. The world tends to be ordered. Things arise in certain sequences — seeds give rise to shoots which turn into plants, which put forth flowers, which give rise to seeds. Apples fall from trees, as Sir Isaac Newton noted, in a downward, not an upward direction. Observing facts such as these, people have, at different times, deduced certain laws which seem to describe the way in which the world works.

An early branch of Buddhist thought divided conditionality into five levels, or orders[1] — the physical, or inorganic, the biological, the psychological, the ethical and the transcendental[2]. Western science, concerned with the objective world, has tended to focus its attentions on the first three levels. Buddhism, on the other hand, concerned above all with what people can do to change themselves for the better, has always taken a more human-centred approach and has tended to focus its attention on the last three levels.

We are familiar with the idea that the physical, biological and psychological dimensions of life are to some extent rule-governed. Scientists may never be able to deduce the final, absolute laws which govern these dimensions, but they can make increasingly accurate predictions based on the laws they hypothesize. What is new to Western thinking is the Buddhist idea that ethics and spiritual development are also governed by universal laws. The ethical dimension is governed by the laws of karma and the higher dimensions of spiritual development are governed by the transcendental order of conditionality. Since the latter is not of immediate, practical import, I shall not be dealing with it any further (there is a footnote for the more inquisitive reader[3]).

The exact way in which events, physical and mental, in the vast network of conditions which make up the universe affect one another is complex beyond our comprehension. It is therefore tempting to home in on one or two levels of conditionality and try to explain everything in terms of these alone[4]. Orthodox Hinduism asserts that all of one's current life experience is entirely the result of karma generated in previous lives; reductionist physicists try to explain everything in terms of the inorganic level of conditionality; and evolutionary biologists try to account for the emergence of consciousness in purely biological terms. The Principle of Conditionality, however, leads one to favour a more holistic approach. Everything that happens is the outcome, not of a single chain of cause-and-effect operating only at one level, but of a potentially infinite network of conditions operating at one or more of the levels of conditionality. Karma is not the only causal factor in the vast network of circumstances that determine the nature of our current existence, but it is a very important one.

The ethical, or karmic order of conditionality governs the way in which one's voluntary actions help to shape one's destiny. This order refers only to *volitional* actions. Involuntary acts have effects but they do not change one's character. To unintentionally strike one's thumb with a hammer will bring about changes in the biological dimension (pain, acute swelling and discoloration) and the psychological dimension (involuntary exclamation and rapid withdrawal of hand)[5] but it will not have much effect in the ethical dimension. One's character, one's will, and therefore one's trajectory through life, will not be much altered by such an action. Intentionally striking someone else with a hammer, on the other hand, has much more serious consequences. It would change one's state of mind very much for the worse and significant negative effects would follow. The ethical outcome of any act depends upon the intention behind it.

In order to understand how this process works, we have first to look more closely at the nature of consciousness itself and at the relationship between ourselves and the world we inhabit.

Buddhism offers a resolution to a problem which has bedevilled Western thought at least since the time of Descartes. What is the relationship between perceiver and perceived? In confronting this riddle, mainstream Western thinkers have tended to stress either one or the other side of the supposed polarity. Is there an objectively existing world which impinges its data on the passive, neutral sense organs of the separate, perceiving subject?

Classical Western empiricism would suggest that there is. All true knowledge is derived from 'objective' data. This view has powered the Western scientific advances of the last two hundred years and it continues to be the dominant, if usually unconscious, presupposition of most scientists. Alternatively, there is the tradition of subjective idealism. Sensing the power of the mind, subjective idealists have seen external phenomena exclusively as mental projections. 'It's all in the mind,' as we used to say in the psychedelic era — a view which often leads to solipsism and social irresponsibility. But neither of these approaches give an adequate account of the nature of the perceiving self and its relationship to its perceptions.

Can the self really be said to have an independent existence? Even a cursory introspection shows us that our experience is always changing and is always dependent on a particular situation. To be alive is to be in a context — a world — and we have no experience that is independent of such a context. The classical assertion of this position from the Western tradition was made by David Hume:

For my part, when I enter most intimately into what I call myself, I stumble on some particular perception or other, of heat or cold, light or shade, love or hatred, pain or pleasure. I never catch myself at any time without a perception, and never can observe anything but the perception.[6]

When we examine our actual experience in any depth, we find nothing more than fleeting transformations of context-dependent sensations. We can find no 'self' which stands somehow apart from these. On the other hand, our sense of being somehow 'located', of occupying a single location within experience, leads us to believe that we have a fixed, unitary self-hood. We have a personality, memories, plans and anticipations which appear to cohere in a single point of view, a single locus from which we stand and survey the world about us. How could such a point of view be possible if it were not rooted in a single, independent, truly existing self or ego? It's a puzzle.

All of the reflective traditions in history — philosophy, science, psychoanalysis, religion, meditation — have challenged the naive sense of self. None of them has ever claimed to discover an independent, fixed or unitary self within the world of experience.[7] But neither do they give an adequate account of the real nature of selfhood. Hume, for example, resigned to his inability to find the self, chose to withdraw and immerse himself in a game of backgammon instead.

The reason for this failure is that the problem is not merely theoretical. Introspection and reflection may well reveal the self to be a context-dependent illusion but intellectual understanding does not, of itself, dispel spiritual ignorance. We may think we have understood the illusory nature of the self, but our instinctive, un-Enlightened nature continually causes us to behave as if the self was real, fixed and separate. Spiritual ignorance, the deep, instinctive attachment to self-hood, is the cause of all suffering. The Buddhist analysis of consciousness is therefore concerned, above all, with seeing how this sense of a fixed and separate self-hood comes into being and how it can be overcome in practice.

Before considering this analysis in more depth, however, we must address the question of rebirth, for we don't always experience the results of our karma immediately — they may come to us much later, even in future lives. Buddhists throughout the ages have taught that the process of re-becoming, the way we re-make ourselves from moment to moment in dependence upon our volitional actions, applies not only to this life. Even beyond the apparent barrier of death our volitions continue and determine the manner in which we are reborn.

Some Western Buddhists are sceptical about the idea of rebirth, maintaining that, given the lack of empirical evidence, we should remain agnostic on the issue. Others argue that, although scant, there is *some* evidence, empirical or otherwise, to support the case for rebirth:[8] there are a variety of scientific studies of the issue; instances of hypnotic regression; the involuntary recollection of details about past lives; near-death experiences; and cases of child prodigies, such as Mozart, who could play and compose at the age of four. They therefore maintain that there is more evidence (albeit slight) for a continuation of consciousness after death than there is for its cessation which, by definition, is not a fact amenable to empirical determination. Death is not an event in life.

We have become who we are largely through the functioning of habit. Our volitional tendencies have pulled together all the different factors floating in the sea of conditions which have gone into making us what we are. The food we tend to eat, the exercise we tend to take, the friends we make, the books we read, the discussions we like to have, the places we are drawn to — all these factors, floating in the sea of conditions, are pulled into a common, fluctuating centre: oneself. The volitional drive which shapes us is very strong. Why should it disperse with death? Why not just carry on, all over again? The proposition that the volitions which determine the way in which one's consciousness is shaped continue to do so after one's death is, on the face of it, no more preposterous than the opposite, apparently 'scientific', assertion: that somehow, out of nothing, one's consciousness came into being for the first time at one's birth.

One can view the Buddhist idea of rebirth from two perspectives: it can mean literal rebirth, a re-becoming after physical death; or one can take it to mean the process by which one's apparent 'self' dies and is reborn from moment to moment as the conditions within and about one change. One moment we are angry and the world seems a bitter place with events continually ranged against us. The next moment the sun comes out, the world brightens, our anger evaporates and it is as if one is an entirely different person living in an entirely different world.

> For we are all insulted by
> The mere suggestion that we die
> Each moment and that each great I
> Is but a process in a process
> Within a field that never closes;
> As proper people find it strange
> That we are changed by what we change,
> That no event can happen twice
> And that no two existences
> Can ever be alike; we'd rather
> Be perfect copies of our father,
> Prefer our idées fixes to be
> True of a fixed reality...[9]

Whatever stand one takes on the subject, it is important to note that rebirth is not the same as reincarnation. The idea of reincarnation suggests that one has a definite 'soul' – an essential nature, which, after death, continues fundamentally unchanged and comes in time to inhabit a new body. Rebirth is better likened to the process whereby a flame burns through a stack of twigs. From moment to moment the flame is always changing, the burning twigs are always changing, and there is no flame apart from the twigs. Just as fire passes from one twig to the next, so our volitional tendencies move our changing consciousness from one shifting existential situation to the next and there is no ultimate separation between consciousness and the existential situation in which it occurs.

There are twelve steps in the Buddhist analysis of this process, beginning with the recognition of the current state of affairs – out of spiritual ignorance[10] we maintain wrong views. Not recognizing the impermanent, insubstantial and intrinsically unsatisfactory nature of things, we deeply believe that we will be able to achieve lasting satisfaction if only we can get what we want.

'If only... it would rain/it wouldn't rain ... I had a job/I didn't have a job ... I was in France/I was not in France ... I had a garden/I didn't have to look after this garden ... I won the lottery/I hadn't won the wretched lottery in the first place ... I was married/I was single ... then I'd really be happy!'

This spiritual ignorance is the basis of our fundamental propensities[11] — memories, expectations and habits — which, carried forward from the past, determine our current mode of consciousness[12].

Consciousness is always embodied[13], the idea of a disembodied mind is just that — an idea — with no counterpart in reality, although the exact nature of that embodiment is not restricted to the human form. Buddhism recognizes the existence of many different modes consciousness, some more, some less refined than the human state.

Consciousness is also always consciousness 'of' something; in the case of human beings, what we are conscious of will be the product of one or more of the six senses[14] (mind is the sixth sense in Buddhist thought).

The nature of our senses conditions the nature of our contact[15] with the objects of experience. I, for example, am red-green blind. The world as I perceive it is therefore significantly different from the one that most people perceive. Perceptions give rise to feelings[16]. Every sensation, thought, memory or emotion has a corresponding feeling-tone which may be pleasant, painful or neutral.

Thus far, all the links in the chain are the inevitable outcome of past events. The nature of the present moment of consciousness, the way in which we perceive the current situation and the feeling-tone which accompanies it is the result of what we have done in the past. Being the outcomes of past events, there is nothing we can do to change them. They are simply given. This is a very important point, for a great deal of energy is wasted in bemoaning the present — 'Why are things like this? Why can't they be different?' This is futile. The present moment cannot be changed. The future, however, can be altogether different. It all depends upon how one acts at this point. For this stage in the process is the one where we generate fresh karma.

Most often, we respond to the feeling-tone of any situation with craving[17] in the case of pleasant feelings, or aversion in the case of unpleasant ones. Craving leads to grasping[18] and attachment. What we cling to shapes us in a particular way[19], and thus a new existential situation is born[20]. And this in turn passes away — moments die, situations die, ways of being die, lives end[21].

The stage in this analysis where feelings give way to craving or aversion has been referred to as the battleground of the spiritual life. Consider an illustration of the sort of thing that sometimes happens at this point:

I used to be given to regularly reading computer magazines. I would say to myself (and those friends that asked) 'The world of computers is changing so quickly, and it affects us all so deeply, you've to keep up with it all.' But really it was just a case of my looking for a bit of semi-innocent titillation, something to distract my attention for a while. I say 'semi-innocent', because computer magazines are not really designed to communicate information about developments in information technology — not altogether. What they're really designed to do is to inculcate techno-lust: a very serious condition. If they didn't do that successfully, then advertisers wouldn't pay and the magazines wouldn't exist.

This is how the process works: I would find myself idly leafing through a computer magazine and then quietly, almost surreptitiously, something would hook. A switch would trip in my mind somewhere, and I'd begin to feel really dissatisfied. 'You know, my current computer, with so many megabytes of RAM and such and such a processor... it's not really good enough. I could do so much better, work so much faster and more efficiently if I had one of those new models, with a more powerful processor...' And gradually, step-by-step, my world would be taken over by this new desire. I'd try to put it aside — 'Come on. Don't be silly. My current machine is fine. It does what I want. Forget about it.' But techno-lust is never rational. It's an itch that takes hold of that part of us which feels somehow incomplete. 'If only I had that machine, then I'd be really happy, then I'd be able to clear my backlog of work and get on with real living...' and I'd find myself in quiet moments building little fantasies about how to find the money for the new machine, or leafing through magazines, trying to find the best deal going. And my desire for the new machine would build and build and build until it seemed that the only way to assuage it was to go out and buy the wretched thing.

From a spiritual perspective, nothing substantial was changed in this process. Spiritual ignorance persists. Old habits were simply continued, the same old wheel simply turned another round. What a waste.

That tiny fraction of a moment, where my mind moved from idly taking in the information in the magazine to actually desiring a new computer set in train a whole course of events which had me in their thrall. By the time craving has moved on to grasping one has set another karmic impulse loose upon the world — the genie is out of the bottle and will never really go back into it. Through a strong act of will one can avoid taking the situation to its ultimate consummation (I could strongly grit my teeth and just refrain from buying that wretched machine—eventually the lust would die down) but that can only happen if one has the space to become sufficiently aware of the process one is engaged in. Most often, one is so preoccupied by the unfolding situation that one only becomes aware of what one is doing at the end of the process. A new consciousness dawns at the moment of birth, as it were, and one realizes what one has done, what one has become. By then, of course, it is too late. The deed is done, a new situation has come into being and one will have to live with its consequences.

What has happened here (as happens everywhere) is that self and the world have been involved in a mutually conditioning process. From the moment that craving clicked into place in my mind, the world I inhabited started to be shaped in a new way by the impulses that followed. Previously, perhaps, I had been living in a more or less human world. Now I started to live in a world dominated by techno-lust. This is a very different world. Its inhabitants think mainly in terms of RAM, ROM, megahertz and megabytes. They disparage last year's technology and yearn for this year's. Their conversation is both arcane and intensely boring and their reading matter is largely confined to computer mail-order advertisements, whose copious information they mechanically scan, digest and compare. Their other sensory apparatus is equally confined. They don't taste their food, for example, and they don't see much at all — when walking in a city, for example, the only thing really able to take their attention is a shop window with computers on display in it. It is a narrow, confined, bleak world and there is little real contact between its inhabitants.

Some occupants of this world find themselves in it only briefly, perhaps for a few days or a week, but there are long-term inhabitants, their hair lank and greasy, their eyes dull and staring. They are able to recite from memory the cost and specifications of most current computer systems and their predominant emotional state is one of dulled, suppressed pain.

The Buddhist tradition enumerates six different worlds which, between them, describe the principal states within which consciousness manifests. The world of techno-lust is not unlike the realm of the hungry ghosts, whose inhabitants are racked by insatiable desires. They have huge, swollen bellies, narrow distended necks and their mouths are no more than pin-pricks. Their bellies are filled with fire and they can never take in enough water to quench the flames, or they may be consumed with aching hunger but what little food they can take in turns to ashes in their mouths.

There are hell realms, where beings suffer unspeakable torments, sunk in pits of excrement, pierced with swords, dismembered, burnt and flayed. Beings arise in this state as a consequence of extremely depraved behaviour such as patricide, matricide and murder. It is a state of acute anguish, suffering and depravity.

The animal realm contains all the animals we know (including some human beings). It is a world of bovine contentment, whose inhabitants are preoccupied only with food, sex and sleep.

There are god realms, states of extreme refinement and aesthetic enjoyment and there is the world of the titans or anti-gods who, not satisfied with what they have of the good things of life, believe that they can get more if only they can exert enough force.

And finally there is the human realm, much cherished in Buddhist thought. The human realm is marked by a kind of centrality. It is a state of relative ethical freedom: not as dominated by a single prevailing state as the other realms. In it we experience both pleasure and pain; we have access to refinement and to suffering; moments of neurosis and moments of slothfulness. We can experience anger but we can also experience love. The human realm is marked by an ability to move between mental states. And so it is a state in which we can fairly easily choose to act so as to change ourselves for the better.

Our propensities, conditioned by spiritual ignorance, deter-mine our current mode of consciousness with its perceptual apparatus. The sensations which arise from these are accompanied by feelings, to which we tend to respond with craving or aversion. This leads to grasping, becoming, birth, death and so on — round and round. But we have a choice. Rather than moving automatically from feeling to craving, we can, given enough awareness, consider the real facts of the matter. For what is it that drives this relentless process of re-becoming?

Our sense of having a real, fixed, separate selfhood is fundamentally delusive. It has no counterpart in reality. Intuiting this fact, always experiencing ourselves as somehow incomplete, we suffer from a sense of existential insecurity which causes us to want to remain within the limits of known experience — to repeat apparently predictable experiences. Striving to bolster our insecure sense of ourselves we reach out for what seems pleasant and thrust away what seems to threaten. This process causes us to cycle endlessly through existence, taking embodiment now in one, now in another existential situation. But all of these different existential states are intrinsically unstable and unsatisfactory — they are all equally 'unreal'.

We can begin to move from unreality towards reality only by being willing and able to confront the real facts of the matter. All the worlds of cyclic existence delineated above are marked by the same fundamental characteristics: they are all impermanent, insubstantial and unable to provide lasting satisfaction. By maintaining an awareness of the intrinsically unsatisfactory nature of the pleasant, painful or neutral feelings which accompany any set of sensations one can, if one is sufficiently aware, at least for a while, choose not to give way to craving or aversion. Instead one can simply maintain a calm awareness of what one is feeling — be it pleasant, painful or neutral. Attending fully to one's current experience, temporarily suspending the urge to move away from it towards some other experience where the grass promises somehow to be greener, a new quality of being emerges and another trajectory through life opens out before one.

This sense of the essentially unsatisfactory nature of mundane experience gives way to confidence: one is no longer quite so deluded, no longer quite so caught up in the futile processes of consumption and rejection. This loosens one's attachment to delusion and one senses the beginnings of real freedom. This intuitive prefiguration of liberative insight gives rise to feelings of joy and happiness. Indeed, one characterization of the Buddhist path suggests that so long as one can maintain one's awareness these feelings, in turn, are followed by a sequence of increasingly positive mental states: rapture, serenity, bliss, and one-pointedness, culminating ultimately in insight into the true nature of reality and spiritual liberation[22].

There are then two fundamental processes. There is the wheel of cyclic existence, where one delusive state gives way to another in an endless round, dominated always by craving, aversion and delusion. And there is a path with spirals up from the wheel through more and more intensely positive mental states.

That is the course of the Buddhist spiritual life. At times one is caught up on the wheel, moving blindly from one existential situation to the next, driven by craving and aversion. At other times one escapes the wheel for a while, maintains a higher degree of awareness and makes some progress along the spiral before falling back onto the wheel again. But over time, as one circles about the wheel, one does it at successively higher, more refined levels. As spiritual practice deepens one's awareness and strengthens one's positive emotions, so one becomes more and more at home in the gap between feeling and craving.

To be in that gap is to have some experience of the open dimension. It is the locus of all creativity. For all creative activities involve a move from the known into the unknown. They require a willingness to leave behind all the habitual responses out of which we build our sense of ourselves and demand instead a capacity for self-transcendence. The change in orientation from the known towards the unknown is the fundamental act of the Buddhist spiritual life. In orienting oneself towards that which lies over the horizon of one's current experience one makes a commitment to the unknown: a commitment to stepping over the edge of one's current experience. The whole of Buddhist practice is concerned solely with this object. It is a training in all the different means of maintaining and orientation towards the open dimension.

Over the centuries Buddhism has devised innumerable practices to support this end. Training in ethical conduct and meditation, contemplation on the nature of reality and devotional practice: all these are designed to wake one up to what is really going on; to help one to stand, eventually unsupported, within the open dimension — free, independent, fully creative; able to respond appropriately, out of the fullness wisdom and compassion, to whatever events one encounters.

---

1. See for example *Atthasalini* by Buddhaghosa, translated as *The Expositor* by Maung Tin, ed. Mrs. Rhys-Davids, Pali Text Society, 1920. Vol. II pg. 360.

2. Pali - *Utu-niyama, Bija-niyama, Citta-niyama, Kamma-niyama, Dhamma-niyama.*

3. The transcendental order of conditionality describes the conditions under which those who have achieved transcendental insight live out their lives from the time of attaining such insight until the time of their achieving complete Buddhahood. See for example the descriptions of the different *Bodhisattva Bhumis* in Mahayana and Vajrayana literature, and of the different levels of the *Arya Sangha* in the Pali scriptures. These can be followed up further in Sangharakshita, *A Survey of Buddhism*, Windhorse Publications, 1993.

4. See Robin Cooper, *The Evolving Mind: Buddhism, Biology and Consciousness,* Windhorse Publications, 1996.

5. Note that the psychological dimension in this categorisation refers to *involuntary* psycho-physical responses.

6. David Hume, *A Treatise of Human Nature*, I, VI, iv.

7. Varela, Thompson and Rosch, *The Embodied Mind*, MIT Press, 1992.

8. Martin Willson, *Re-birth and the Western Buddhist*, Wisdom Publications, 1984.

Sangharakshita, *Who is the Buddha?*, Windhorse Publications, 1994.

9. W.H. Auden, 'New Year Letter' (January 1, 1940), *W.H. Auden Collected Longer Poems*, Faber and Faber, 1968.

10. Ignorance, *Avidya.*

11. Propensities (Karma Formations), *Samskarah.*

12. Consciousness, *Vijnana.*

13. Name and Form (Body and Mind), *Nama-rupa.*

14. The Six Senses, *Sadayatana.*

15. Contact, *Sparsa.*

16. Feeling, *Vedana.*

17. Craving, *Trsna.*

18. Grasping, *Upadana.*

19. Becoming, *Bhava.*

20. Birth, *Jati.*

21. Decay and Death, *Jara-marana.*

22. This is a slightly truncated version of the Spiral Path. C.A.F. Rhys Davids, *The Book of Kindred Sayings* Vol. II, p. 27 gives one of the more poetically beautiful renderings of the processes of the Wheel and Spiral to be found in the Pali Canon. See also Sangharakshita *A Survey of Buddhism* and *The Three Jewels* for a fuller working out of this whole schema.

Chapter 4

Going for Refuge: Commitment

The philosopher says *cogito* — I think; the Christian says *credo* — I believe; the Buddhist says *gacchami* — I go.[1]

Buddhism is essentially voluntarist: it is concerned not so much with what one believes as with what one wills. Beliefs are important only in so far as they affect how one acts, and Buddhism maintains that all beliefs are ultimately provisional. They have value only in as much as they help us to move onward towards Enlightenment. As we progress along the path our views and beliefs will inevitably change. Eventually, as we saw in *The Parable of the Raft*, they will all have to be discarded. Buddhism is therefore concerned more with one's fundamental orientation — one's basic trajectory through life — than with one's beliefs (although one's beliefs will both reflect and affect that basic orientation).

> *Buddham saranam gacchami*
> *Dhammam saranam gacchami*
> *Sangham saranam gacchami*
>
> *To the Buddha for Refuge I go!*
> *To the Dharma for Refuge I go!*
> *To the Sangha for Refuge I go!*

This threefold refuge formula, which is used throughout the Buddhist world, expresses the Buddhist aspiration to orient one's life around the Buddha, the Dharma and Sangha — the Three Jewels — the three highest ideals of Buddhism.

The word 'refuge' can at first seem a little problematic. It has connotations of escapism, of taking shelter from the facts of life, but in the context of the Three Refuges it means the exact opposite. To take refuge in the Buddha means to take refuge in reality, in how things really are. Most of the time, most of us take refuge in delusion, for the process of taking refuge is endemic to the human condition.

There are no essences. We have no fixed self-hood. Everything always changes. We respond to this chaos by trying to bring order and stability to our lives, trying to pin things down, but no sooner have we got one area of our lives under control than another area begins to change. Everything we try to grasp hold of slips in the end from our fingers. In the face of this we naturally look for a point of stability: something to rely on and organize our lives around — something to give us our bearings amidst the dilemmas and confusion of daily life.

For most of us, one of our first refuges is our own physical body. In the midst of the flux of change it at least seems somewhat solid and permanent. Our bodies change only gradually, more or less imperceptibly. To be alive is to have a body and, from the way our senses work, we get the impression that our mind is somehow firmly located within it. Our bodies give us a sense of having a single, unified identity — 'Me,' we say, pointing to our body. We preen our bodies, pamper and adorn them, make sure they are comfortable, and, by whatever possible means, we strive to forget that, like everything else, our bodies are ultimately impermanent. Eventually the body will sicken and we will die. The body is not a safe refuge.

Some people go for refuge to their careers, putting their job ahead of all other considerations. 'I'd like to look after my elderly mother, but I really can't. I've got my career to think about.' Going for refuge to one's career gives one a sense of a hierarchy of values to live by. It begins to crystallize meaning and order out of the chaos of all the multiple possibilities which modern life presents.

We take refuge in our lovers, husbands or wives; in our families; in the things we own; in the things we do — all these give us a sense of meaning and identity. We put enormous amounts of energy into erecting bulwarks against change and we do this because we have an intuition of the terrifying fact of universal emptiness. We fear the open dimension: we would rather it were closed. Then the chill breeze of existential change would be shut out and we could settle down to a warm, cosy predictability — we would know who we are, what we should do and we would be safe.

Whenever the open dimension begins to make itself felt, even a little, we run for cover. We do something, anything, to distract ourselves, to turn our attention away from the uncomfortable facts of impermanence and insubstantiality. The strategies that we employ in the face of even the slightest impingement of the open dimension are legion. One very common manifestation is the 'chocolate crisis'. Many of us experience this and it has made some of the shareholders in Western confectionery companies very wealthy.

It goes like this: I'm doing something fairly ordinary — perhaps I'm working at my desk, and I begin to get the very first hint of a feeling that something is wrong in my life. Something is missing. I don't know what it is, but there is something not quite right just at the moment — there is something unsatisfied, something I'm not getting... This feeling begins to grow, it starts to become clearer, and then suddenly it manifests in all its glorious completeness: what I need is a bar of chocolate! That's what I need. That will put an end to my feeling of unsatisfactoriness.

So I put my work aside, take a break, and trot down to the corner shop where I part with some small change in exchange for the magical panacea which is going to put an end to my sense of unsatisfactoriness — quite possibly forever — and, fully confident in its magical powers, I strip it of its red and white paper wrapper, rid it of its shimmering silver foil, pop it into my mouth and what happens?

Not a lot. I get a slightly sickly aftertaste and a little *frisson* of guilt from having unnecessarily put on all that extra weight. Taking refuge in a bar of chocolate in the face of universal emptiness is no way to reconcile oneself to reality.

This is not to say that there is anything intrinsically wrong with eating chocolate. It can, after all, have physiologically beneficial effects: it can give one a boost of energy; it has caffeine to promote alertness and other chemicals which promote a kind of mild euphoria, and Buddhism has nothing against pleasure and sensory enjoyment. Distinctions are important here. There are innocuous and insidious pleasures (as we shall see in the section on ethics) and there are wholesome and neurotic desires. Neurosis is the attempt the use to use one experience in order to repress another: to grasp onto something in order to avoid facing up to something else.

The most wholesome desire is the desire for truth, something which every human being has to a certain extent. One might even say that neurotic desire is the distorted shadow of this more primary, liberating, wholesome desire. Nonetheless, to be un-Enlightened is to be dominated by desires which keep us entrapped, desires which are intrinsically neurotic because their ends can never be fulfilled. Lovers, careers, cars, families, television, bars of chocolate: none of these can keep the winds of change at bay, none can fill the space which is, in fact, the open dimension itself. They cannot change the existential facts of impermanence, insubstantiality, and intrinsic unsatisfactoriness.

Yet we have to order our lives somehow or else we would be swept away by the chaotic whirl of events. Consciously or unconsciously, we all work to shape our lives somehow or other all the time. The pattern and shape of our lives, our behaviour, our values: all these indicate what we take refuge in.

Rather than try to hide from the truth of things, Buddhists take refuge in the truth itself. They take refuge in the Buddha, who discovered and embodies the highest truth; in the Dharma, his teaching of the truth; and in the Sangha, all those men and women who have made that truth their own.

In some parts of the East, taking refuge in the Buddha has come to mean seeking his help by way of intercessionary prayer. Students pray to the Buddha for help with their exams, women pray for the birth of a son, young men for an advance in their careers. Whatever the value of such practices, a very different interpretation of the meaning of Going for Refuge emerges from the earliest Buddhist scriptures. Here there is an explicit correlation between going for refuge and the act of spiritual commitment.

The early texts often describe someone meeting the Buddha for the first time. They enter into discussion and that person is so overwhelmed by the Buddha's presence, his understanding and insight, that they say something like this:

Excellent, Lord! Excellent it is, Lord! Just as if one should raise what is overthrown, or show forth what is hidden, or point the way to him who wanders astray, or hold up a light in the darkness that they who have eyes may see object — even so in divers ways has the Dharma been set forth by the Venerable Gotama. To the Venerable Gotama I Go for Refuge, to the Dharma, and to the Sangha from this day on so long as life lasts.[2]

Their whole world has been rearranged, the course of their life changed and they commit themselves to following the spiritual path that the Buddha's teachings opened up for them.

I remember the moment when something like this first happened in my own life. Internally, it was both sudden and dramatic but externally, I doubt whether anyone could have seen what had happened. I was studying philosophy at university and one of my tutors, who knew that I had an interest in Buddhism, invited me around to his house to meet a man he had staying with him — a Western Buddhist. I duly went, tea was drunk, and I tried to engage this strange Buddhist in conversation.

'So, tell me about the Void then.'

'Oh... well... I don't think I know anything about that...'

'Humph...' I thought, 'not much of a Buddhist!' And that was going to be the end of it — I thought.

A few days later I was walking along the road and this same Buddhist came walking towards me. I stopped. He stopped.

'Hello,' I said.

'Hello,' he said.

And I was totally astonished.

I realized, in a flash of intuition, that what was happening in our communication was something that had never happened with me, ever before.

Here was another human being, simply, confidently and openly, just being himself. He wanted nothing from me and had no desire that I should see him any particular way. He was happy simply to be himself and he was happy for me simply to be myself. How extraordinary! I knew for certain, in that moment, that whatever this man was doing that allowed him to be like that, I wanted it too. He was a member of the Western Buddhist Order. I too would become a member of that Order. And so, a year or so later, I did[3].

To go for refuge to the Buddha is to aspire to awaken one's own highest potential. In a sense, human beings have Buddhahood enfolded within them. In the same way acorns have oak trees enfolded in them. But not every acorn becomes an oak tree — few human beings become a Buddha. Acorns become oak trees only in dependence upon the right conditions: some fall on stony ground, some are eaten by squirrels. Even if they germinate and begin to grow, very few oak saplings eventually become oak trees. Of all the hundreds of thousands of acorns produced by any oak tree over the course of its life only a very few become fully grown trees.

Even fewer humans become Buddhas. Nonetheless, in going for refuge to the Buddha one commits oneself to becoming more than one is now. By creating the conditions which help one to develop — to unfold more of one's potential for creativity and understanding — one sets out on a path of self-transcendence that has no limit. We hardly know who we are now let alone who, with the right effort, we might become.

To go for refuge to the Buddha is to commit oneself to leaving behind all one's fixed views of oneself. One tries to let go of the false security of ego-identity and to orient oneself instead towards the open dimension. For, given the right kind of effort, one thing is assured: you can become more than you are now — every one of us has the capacity to experience some degree of transcendental, liberating insight.

Dharma is a complex Sanskrit word. It can mean truth, law, mental event, doctrine or spiritual path. In the context of the Three Refuges, however, it means the Buddha's teachings and all those communications of the Enlightened mind which point out the way to liberation.

'If you can be sure,' the Buddha once said, 'that a teaching leads to calm, not to agitation; to freedom, not to attachment; to moderation, not to covetousness; to content, not to discontent; to independence, not to dependence; to energy, not to indolence; to delight in good, not depravity — then you can be sure that it is the Dharma.'⁴ The Dharma is whatever helps one along the path of self-transcendence.

At another time, a group of young men came to see the Buddha to ask for his advice. They were living at a time that was in many ways like our own. The old order was breaking down and radical new ideas, especially in the field of religious doctrine, were being propagated. Bewildered by the various conflicting claims of the priests and holy men who preached different doctrines (and spent much of the time bickering with one another), they asked the Buddha how they themselves might adjudicate between these various claims.

The Buddha replied, 'Don't just go by what is said — what your people and your traditions maintain. Nor can you rely solely on reason, inference or argument, for this is not only at matter of opinion. Nor should you take anything on simply out of respect, thinking that a holy man must be deferred to.

But, when you know, *from your own experience*, that a set of teachings, condemned by the wise, when put into practice conduce to loss and suffering — then reject them.'[5]

Buddhism requires you to reflect on your own experience and form your judgements on the basis of practical experience.

Whoever practises the Dharma is a member of the Sangha. It is one of Buddhism's great strengths that it has at its heart the ideal of spiritual fellowship. But when the term is used in the context of the Three Refuges, the word Sangha refers to the Noble Sangha — all those men and women, throughout time, who have achieved an irreversible degree of spiritual attainment. People of this spiritual calibre are the only truly reliable guides along the path. They have experienced an insight into the nature of reality which has completely reoriented their entire being and their lives are models of selflessness, wisdom, compassion and generosity.

Not all of the members of the Noble Sangha are human. Buddhism also recognizes the existence of archetypal beings. Buddhas and Bodhisattvas[6]: luminous beings who manifest at the interface between Buddhahood and the human imagination. They appear in the sky above the horizon which stands between us and transcendental reality — translucent indications of ever higher levels of being and consciousness.

Traditionally, in the East, there came to be three broad classifications of Sangha: the Noble Sangha[7]; the monastic Sangha — the Order of monks and nuns; and the Greater Sangha[8] — all those men and women, whatever their style of life, who went for Refuge to the Three Jewels. Over time, however, the word increasingly came to be used to refer almost exclusively to the monastic Order, who themselves increasingly came to occupy centre-stage in Buddhist religious life. The consequences of this fact have not always been very happy. It created a vast gulf between the 'religious professionals' and the relatively irreligious laity, and it circumscribed the options for spiritual practice in a lay context to a very high degree. At worst, the layman's part was simply to support the monks whilst the monk's task was simply to appear to be worthy of such support (the Order of nuns having died out in many parts of the Buddhist East).[9]

As Buddhism has come to the West however, different conditions prevail. Since the social changes of the 1960s people in our society are no longer faced with the stark choice between being celibate or being married — a whole range of new social options is being explored and the former, absolute distinctions between monks and laity no longer apply.

In Western Buddhist circles today some of the most committed practice of the Dharma takes place amongst people who, although not strictly speaking monks or nuns, cannot either be described (as previously in the East) simply as householders. Western Buddhism is currently redrawing the boundaries of the Sangha, placing the emphasis back, as it was in the Buddha's day, on the question of commitment and seeing the issue of the lifestyle through which one lives out that commitment as secondary (although by no means unimportant).

Sangha in this sense therefore refers to any spiritual community whose members are effectively committed to the Three Jewels. Such a spiritual community is not a 'group' in the ordinary sense. One of the characteristics of a group in this sense is that it seeks to preserve itself, if necessary at the cost of its individual members. Thus it tends to enforce conformity and to require unquestioning allegiance from its members. The spiritual community, on the other hand, encourages its members not to conform but to become increasingly more individual: to become ever more true to themselves, unfolding more and more of their own, unique, creative potential. The spiritual community encourages its members to always seek out the open dimension; the group always tries to erect bulwarks against it. The group, whether it be a family, clan, tribe, nation, club, race, team, squadron, church, regiment or political party, comes down, in the end, to a frail conspiracy against the winds of change, blowing from the open dimension.

In Going for Refuge one seeks constantly to reorient oneself — redirecting one's fundamental drives and volitions, ever more radically, from the mundane to the transcendental, from constriction to liberation; for one's own sake and that of all living beings. Every act that moves one along the path is an act of Going for Refuge. When one sits in meditation, turning one's attention, to some degree at least, towards the open dimension, one thereby Goes for Refuge. Whenever one performs a kindly action, turning from self-concern to a concern for others, moving a little bit closer towards a state in which the subject/object duality is transcended, to that extent one Goes for Refuge. Going for Refuge describes the whole volitional process which makes up the Buddhist spiritual path — the effort which all Buddhists make to strive towards Buddhahood, again and again and again.

Since Buddhism suggests that we can all develop, it necessarily follows that some will be more developed than others. All Buddhists try to orient their lives around the Three Jewels. Some do it more effectively than others.

As one advances along the path one Goes for Refuge to a progressively greater extent, one's commitment to the Three Jewels strengthens and the values they embody come to inform one's acts of body, speech and mind at ever deeper levels. There are, therefore, a number of different levels of Going for Refuge.

As a spiritual path, Buddhism begins at the level of 'provisional' Going for Refuge. This is the point at which one decides to make a conscious effort to undertake Buddhist practices for the sake of spiritual development. In contemporary Western Buddhist circles this level comprises quite a broad band of experience. It includes those who are attending their first meditation class and those who, having heard their first lecture on Buddhism, try to apply the teachings to their daily life. It also includes people who may have been practising Buddhism for many years but for whom it is still simply one amongst many other things they do. They attend a Buddhist centre regularly, perhaps even keep up a regular meditation practice, but they also have other occupations and commitments to which they accord equal or even greater priority.

Then there is 'effective' Going for Refuge. This is the level of those people whose commitment to the Three Jewels has become the central, defining characteristic of their lives. They try to place the Three Jewels at the centre of their lives and to orient the rest of their lives around them. In many cases the transition from provisional to effective Going for Refuge is marked by a person's taking ordination and joining a Buddhist order (although ordination is not in itself a guarantee that a person's Going for Refuge is indeed effective). But however it is marked (or even if it is not publicly marked at all), the transition from provisional to effective Going for Refuge consists in an act of spiritual commitment. An act that can have very dramatic consequences:

Until one is committed there is hesitancy, the chance to draw back; always ineffectiveness. Concerning all acts of initiative (and creation), there is one elementary truth, the ignorance of which kills countless ideas and splendid plans: that the moment one definitely commits oneself then Providence moves too.

All sorts of things occur to help one that would never otherwise have occurred. A whole stream of events issues from the decision, raising in one's favour all manner of unforeseen incidents and meetings and material assistance, which no man could have dreamed would come his way.[10]

Whatever you can do, or dream you can do, begin it! Boldness has genius, magic, and power in it. Begin it now![11]

In effectively committing oneself to Going for Refuge one tries to orient oneself towards the open dimension — to embrace unpredictability and change — and one begins to touch upon a magical realm of unforeseeable consequences.

But, exciting as all this may be, at the level of effective Going for Refuge one's progress along the path is still dependent upon conditions. Given the right conditions one will continue to Go for Refuge and advance along the path. But should conditions change, and advantageous conditions give way to adverse ones, then one's progress may cease, one might fall back, one might even abandon one's commitment altogether. Only at the 'real' level of Going for Refuge does progress along the path become irreversible.

The transition from effective to real Going for Refuge is marked by a complete reorientation in the whole of one's being. This may take place over a period of time or it may occur in a single moment, in a flash of insight into the true nature of reality. However it comes about, the defining characteristic of this level of Going for Refuge is that from here on one can no longer fall back. Having experienced, with the whole of one's being, how things really are — that they are impermanent, insubstantial and ultimately unsatisfying — one's attachment to the Wheel is loosened. One escapes the gravitational pull of delusion and, now having a natural urge towards spiritual practice, one progresses inexorably towards the horizon.

Lofty as the state of real Going for Refuge is, it is not the same as Enlightenment. There is still work to do before one's vision fully coincides with that of the Buddha. This happens at the level of 'absolute' Going for Refuge, the achievement of Buddhahood itself.

The goal of Buddhahood, absolute Going for Refuge, can be dauntingly lofty. But spiritual irreversibility, real Going for Refuge, can be achieved in this lifetime by all who make the effort. That effort begins with provisional Going for Refuge which changes in time to effective Going for Refuge. These are the levels at which most Buddhists live out their lives, and progress at these levels depends to a large extent upon the conditions under which one lives. At this level spiritual practice needs supportive conditions in order to bear fruit. Going for Refuge, the will to practise the Dharma, is the primary matter. But lifestyle, the conditions within which that practice takes place, is also crucially important.

Over the last thirty or so years, Western Buddhists have been concerned with the question of developing those styles of life which most effectively conduce to Dharma practice. Some have been quite conservative in their approach, trying to create conditions which allow them to follow the lifestyles which evolved in Asia to support the lives of practitioners in one or another of the many Asian sects and schools. Thus there are men and women, living in the West, following lifestyles which evolved in different ways to support Thai monastics, Japanese Zen priests or Tibetan scholar monks. Other Western Buddhists have been more radical, trying to work out what styles of life are appropriate to supporting effective Going for Refuge under the particular conditions which pertain in the West today. I will describe instances of both of these approaches in Chapter 7.

Before that, however, we need to examine some of the principal practices by means of which Buddhists put their Going for Refuge into effect. One of the most fundamental of these is the practice of ethics. As you do, so you become. Buddhists ethics describes all the different means by which Buddhist practitioners try to bring their actions into line with their aspiration towards real Going for Refuge.

---

1. Sangharakshita—in conversation.

2. *Samyuta Nikaya iv. 305*, quoted in *Some Sayings of the Buddha*, Woodward, Buddhist Society, 1974 (amended).

3. The man I had met was my good friend Devamitra, to whom I am forever grateful. And in those days ordination training in the Western Buddhist Order was a much briefer affair than it is today.

4. Adapted from *Vinaya II.10*.

5. Adapted from *Anguttara-Nikaya* I-188.

6. Bodhisattvas (the last word I'll leave untranslated), are beings set upon Enlightenment, not only for their own sake, but for that of all living beings.

7. *Arya Sangha.*

8. *Maha-Sangha.*

9. See Sangharakshita, *Forty-Three Years Ago*, Windhorse Publications, Glasgow 1993, for a more detailed discussion of this issue.

10. W.H. Murray, *The Scottish Himalayan Expedition*, Dent, 1951.

11. Attributed to Goethe. But I cannot find the source.

Chapter 5

Buddhist Ethics

Have you not heard of that madman who lit a lantern in the bright morning hours, ran to the market place, and cried incessantly: 'I seek God! I seek God!' ... 'Where is God?' he cried; 'I will tell you. We have killed him—you and I. All of us are his murderers. But how did we do this? ... Who gave us the sponge to wipe away the entire horizon? ... God is dead. God remains dead. And we have killed him ... There has never been a greater deed; and whoever is born after us — for the sake of this deed will belong to a higher history than all history before.'[1]

Thus wrote Nietzsche in 1882. Truly, there have been fewer events in Western history more significant than the death of God. No aspect of our culture has been unaffected by it, and although we may not mourn God's passing, perhaps we can see that with his death we have lost something else as well. We have wiped away 'the entire horizon'. The seemingly impermeable dividing line between God and Man, heaven and earth, the sacred and the secular — that has gone too — and with it the vertical dimension has gone out of life. We have come to live on a horizontal plane of value where nothing is worth very much more than anything else.

At least as far back as the time of Plato, Western man divided the universe in two: the real and the apparent, the transcendental and the mundane, the absolute and the relative. Man, living at the level of the mundane, derived his values from the transcendental. Morality was what God commanded:

And the Lord said unto Moses, come up to me into the mount, and be there: and I will give thee tablets of stone, and a law, and commandments which I have written; that thou mayest teach them.

But now the horizon is gone. We still have the church but, at least in the industrialized West, it has nothing like its former moral or spiritual authority.

Moral certainty began to die with the passing of the Victorian era and it has been fading ever since. To our modern, sophisticated eyes, the old Victorian convictions, values which powered the creation of a vast and confident Empire, seem somehow naive and uninformed. We know more than that now. For the Victorians, bigamy was clearly an abomination. The Bible told them so, and those cultures which practised bigamy, polygamy or polyandry, thereby displayed their cultural inferiority. Such brute heathens were self-evidently in need of the civilizing influence of one of the many Victorian missionary societies.

We can't think like that today. We've seen, read and travelled too much. We know that different people do things differently, and in the pluralistic, multi-cultural modern West the tolerance which such sophistication affords us is no bad thing. But it is tolerance bought at a price. For we now face a peculiarly modern dilemma. Having wiped away the horizon between God and Man, we have also begun to lose the distinction between certainty and bigotry, conviction and prejudice.

History appears to teach us that those who claim to be in possession of some unique truth which gives them moral authority tend to impose their will on others. Our history is a history of religious wars and ideological conflicts. From the Crusaders to the Khmer Rouge, atrocity and dogma have gone hand in hand, and we have come to believe that anyone who claims to know the absolute truth of things will inevitably be driven to impose their beliefs on others — by force if necessary.

We have moved from recognizing that absolutist claims have often led to tyranny to a belief that all claims to truth inevitably lead to tyranny, and this has led us to a widespread scepticism in the whole area of moral judgement. For who really has the right to stand in judgement over anyone else? *We* may believe that eating people is wrong, but can we foist our own beliefs on cultures where cannibalism has long been the norm?

For where can one stand to judge from? When God went out of the picture we also lost the one fixed point in a shifting world. Now that we know just how much our views and opinions are simply the products of our particular upbringing — determined as much as anything by the views of our parents, our class, our nation and our culture — what confidence can we have in their validity? If all our judgements are merely expressions of the cultural norms we have inherited, then there is no single, value-free, objective standpoint from where we can cast a clear and unbiased eye upon the world about us. From this perspective, all our judgements can easily be seen as nothing more than the expression of our particular prejudices, and to make a judgement is simply to be 'judgmental': something decent people are definitely not supposed to be these days.

It is a problem. We cannot, nor would we want to, go back. The politicians cry for 'a return to basics', their espousal of 'family values' have been revealed, time and again, for what they are — a hollow sentimentalism, with nothing meaningful to offer our modern conundrum.

The old public certainties have been reduced to the status of private opinion and the values which for so long lent coherence to social life are fast disappearing. We stand on a cliff's edge, watching the sea eat away the very ground beneath our feet. The Sea of Faith, which once 'lay like the folds of a bright girdle' around earth's shore, and whose 'melancholy, long withdrawing roar' Matthew Arnold so lamented, has given way to the Sea of Scepticism.

As the old value consensus collapses, two broad strands of opinion emerge. On the apparently liberal wing are the postmoderns. From their standpoint, the only valid judgements one can make are those which *level*. To say that Shakespeare was one of the greatest ever poets is no longer allowable. It puts him too much on a pedestal and betrays one's masculinist Eurocentrism. To dismiss him as simply another Dead White European Male is, on the other hand, allowed, for it knocks him off his marble pedestal and evens things out again.

On the other wing are the proponents of free-market individualism who, in the cause of freedom and for the sake of 'market efficiencies', would always leave the weak to be exploited by the strong.

For all their different postures, what both of these stances have in common is that neither of them looks beyond immediate, short-term, material concerns.

Whichever strand of opinion one tends towards, the collapse of a social value-consensus has thrown us back upon ourselves and into states of excessive self-concern. Failing to find reliable

sources of value outside ourselves, we fall back into preoccupation with our subjective mental states in a self-enclosed world
where our own immediate gratification is the only authentic
course open to us. This attitude has rarely been better expressed than in a recent statement in defence of private transport by a British government minister with responsibility for
public transport:

[Cars are extraordinarily convenient because] 'You have your
own company, your own temperature control, your own music –
and you don't have to put up with dreadful human beings sitting
alongside you.'

From smug government ministers in air-conditioned, stereo-
phonic limousines to blank-eyed teenagers plugged into Walk-
mans on public transport, alienation and isolation is the order
of the day. This is the modern malaise.

Can we find a path between the discredited, divine absolute
on the one hand and modern self-enclosed subjectivity on
the other? Is there a way of thinking about ethics and values
which avoids the pitfalls of authoritarianism? Can one speak
of 'higher values' without invoking theism? These questions
go to the heart of the Buddhist approach to values. Can
Buddhism show us a way out of the modern malaise?

Buddhism avoids both poles of the issue. It is non-theistic, but
it doesn't fall back from there into a mono-dimensional
humanism, where current human experience restricts the
boundaries of possibility to a single horizontal plane. There
is a transcendental dimension to Buddhism which can help
us to restore the vertical dimension to our lives but which,
at the same time, is not to be confused with that ghostly
transcendental being who is also our ruler and judge for, as

we have seen, the theist and the Buddhist talk about transcendence in very different ways.

To begin with, they each have a different conception of what is meant by 'faith'. 'In dependence upon suffering, faith arises.' As we have seen, the Buddhist path begins with the recognition that things could be better. This is the fundamental basis of all Buddhist doctrines and methods: it is always possible to move from 'less' to 'more'. Clearly this is a matter of faith. It is not susceptible to logical proof and can only be asserted with reference to one's own, personal experience. But it rigorously takes its stand upon personal experience, and nowhere requires that we simply suspend disbelief and make a 'leap of faith': Buddhists are never enjoined to simply *believe*—there is no Buddhist equivalent of the First Commandment:

I am the Lord thy God ... Thou shalt have no other gods before me ...

for I the Lord thy God am a jealous God, visiting the iniquities of the fathers upon the children unto the third and fourth generation of them that hate me...[2]

Nonetheless, founded upon the simple proposition, verified by our own experience, that it is possible to move from 'less' to 'more', the whole of Buddhism can be unfolded and a vertical dimension to life revealed. For if it is *always* possible to move from 'less' to 'more' then the possibilities of what might constitute 'more' are ultimately limitless and we can begin to imagine a path of personal development which passes entirely beyond the horizon of our current level of being and consciousness.

Buddhism restores the horizon which Nietzsche saw had been wiped away. But it does so without resort to a transcendental divinity. For the horizon is simply the furthest point we can conceive of in the development of consciousness. Enlightenment, Buddhahood, the Transcendental Dimension — call it what you will — are all over that horizon. And the separation between us and Buddhahood is not itself ultimate. We can all become Buddhas. We can, ourselves, begin to move towards and eventually over the horizon, by way of a process of continual self-transcendence.

This process of self-transcendence is the key concept underlying the Buddhist system of values. We suffer because we experience ourselves as limited — constricted within the boundaries of a tight ego-identity which we constantly strive to augment and protect under the threefold compulsion of craving, aversion and delusion. Craving, as we have seen, is the impulse to seek out and try to incorporate into our ego-identity the things that we like in the hope that we will derive security from them; aversion is the impulse to push away from ourselves whatever we dislike or which threatens our ego-identity; and this whole process is driven by the vain delusion that our ego-identity can ever be securely established in the face of a continually changing world. The volitional tendencies which lead us again and again to repeat this kind of profitless behaviour are very deep-seated. They are the cause of all of our own and others' suffering.

No one wants to suffer. We all want happiness. But in seeking happiness by clinging to a restricting ego-identity, again and again we cause ourselves and others to suffer. Such forms of behaviour are therefore intrinsically dysfunctional. In traditional Buddhist terms they are unskilful[3]. Skilful actions, on the other hand, cause us, at least momentarily, to transcend our narrow ego-identity. Generosity, kindness, clarity, aesthetic appreciation — actions based in states such as these lead away from self-preoccupation, towards self-transcendence. They lead us along the path which lies between ourselves and Buddhahood.

All creative acts proceed by way of a move from the known into the unknown, a stepping over the edge, out of our usual habitual rut and into something previously untried. Leaving the known, the safe, the familiar, the habitual, drawn by a sense that more is possible, in any situation we can transcend our previous, limited sense of ourselves and grow larger. In doing so, however temporarily, we enter the open dimension — to that extent and in that moment, transcendence manifests.

This experience of transcendence can be seen from the subjective or from the objective perspective. Both of these viewpoints are just that — viewpoints. Subject and object are not ultimately separate — they are just different aspects of, different perspectives on, reality. From the subjective point of view, transcendence can be seen, more or less psychologically, as self-transcendence. From the objective point of view it is seen, more or less spiritually, as the manifestation of the transcendental dimension of being.

Viewed with the eye of the imagination, the objective perspective on the process of transcendence is epitomized by the figures of the archetypal Buddhas and the Bodhisattvas, beings whose very nature is unending self-transcendence, whilst from a historical point of view it is personified in the figures of Shakyamuni — the human, historical Buddha —and all of the great Enlightened sages of history.

From the perspective of being un-Enlightened, experiencing oneself as a limited ego-identity acting in a world of discrete subjects and objects, one cannot fully conceive the nature of the Buddha's Enlightenment — that state of being which is not limited by attachment to selfhood and which resonates with total compassion for all living beings. But we know, from our own experience, that self-transcendence is possible, and extrapolating from that we can discern a path which leads over the horizon, a path made up of ever-increasing moments of self-transcendence and creativity.

This is the path of the Dharma which was taught by the Buddha. Attracted by the creative possibilities it unfolds, we can set out along that path, emulating those who have gone before us — the Noble Sangha. The orientation towards the open dimension, the process of Going for Refuge to the Three Jewels, the Buddha, the Dharma and the Sangha, means steering always for what is the best in any situation, being willing to go over the edge for the sake of becoming kinder, broader, clearer, wiser.

It is from this orientation towards transcendence that the Buddhist system of values derives. There *is* a hierarchy of values, but it is a hierarchy which is entirely pragmatic. Thoughts, words and deeds which conduce towards self-transcendence are skilful, those that lead away from it are not. This is what Buddhism has to offer the world today. A system of values which leads away from nihilistic self-preoccupation, which continually refers to the transcendental but which is neither authoritarian nor theistic. It is the Middle Way.

An early Buddhist text, the *Karaniya Metta Sutta*, beautifully illustrates this path. It begins conditionally — 'if you know what is really good for you, and want to gain Enlightenment, then you should behave like this' — and it goes on to delineate the path which leads from the cultivation of ethics, to loving kindness and finally perfect wisdom:

> If you know your own good
> and know where peace dwells
> then this is the task:
> lead a simple and frugal life
> uncorrupted, capable and just,
> be mild, speak soft, eradicate conceit,
> keep appetites and sense calm.
> be discrete and unassuming,
> do not seek rewards,
> do not have to be ashamed
> in the presence of the wise.
> May everything that lives be well!
> weak or strong, large or small,
> seen or unseen, here or elsewhere,
> present or to come, in heights or depths.
> have that mind for all the world,
> get rid of lies and pride,
> a mother's mind for her baby,
> her love, but now unbounded.
> secure this mind of love,
> no enemies, no obstructions,
> wherever or however you may be!
> it is sublime, this,
> it escapes birth and death,
> losing lust and delusion,
> and living in the truth![4]

These teachings are more than mere pious sentiments. Their import is fundamentally practical. Although their goal is very lofty (Enlightenment: the transcendence of birth and death) they are based in a simple, practical truth — as we do, so we become.

Buddhist ethics are an ethics of intention. What we are now is the result of our past karma — our previous intentional actions. Few of us consciously set out to become exactly who we now are. Most of us live our lives caught up in a process of blind change — things just seem to happen to us.

Unaware of the true nature of things, we see the world as divided into self and other, and we try to defend the self against incursions from the other, or to augment it by inclusion of the other, all the time. Blinded by spiritual ignorance, dominated by habitual, repetitive urges, we act again and again so as to re-establish familiar but transitory and insubstantial existential situations. Grasping for the pleasant, pushing away the painful, we tread the same familiar paths, over and over, in an endless round of re-becoming — making and re-making our limited selves, our limited worlds, over and over.

We make ourselves. The modern Western tendency is to want to put the responsibility for how we are onto others — parents, schools, siblings, friends, social class and economic forces. We blame men, women, nature, nurture, money or God.

Buddhism, however, takes its stand upon the law of karma. What we are now is the result of what we have done before and, rather than blame anyone or anything for what has transpired, we should just recognize the position we are in and, making positive use of the law of karma, set about trying to improve it. We can consciously set out to change ourselves for the better by creating positive karma: by changing our volitions so that we begin to act in ways which will produce beneficial results for ourselves and others. Buddhism offers us a number of tools to help in this process of changing our volitions. One of the most effective of these is the practice of ethics.

Western history has led us to associate the idea of ethics with a tendency to restrictive anti-liberalism. But the intention of Buddhist ethics is just the opposite: the practice of ethics is an integral part of the path to complete liberation.

Buddhist ethics is not commandment based. Judaeo-Christian ethical systems broadly distinguish between good and evil acts. Good acts are rewarded, evil one's are punished, and the system of reward and punishment is adjudicated by a great cosmic ruler — all-seeing, all-knowing, all-powerful. Buddhist ethics, as we have seen, describes actions as being either skilful or unskilful. Its criteria are not theological but psychological. No act has a value in and of itself, it will be skilful or unskilful depending upon the intention, the mental state, behind it.

There are a host of teaching stories used to illustrate this point:

Once there was a devout hermit, a monk, who lived in solitude near to a village, getting on with his practice of meditation. Every day the same family would provide him with his daily meal. One day, the beautiful daughter of the family brought him his meal and, seeing him deep in meditation, was about to depart when the monk leapt up from his seat and pounced upon her. The frail old hermit was no match for the young farm girl, who fought him off and ran sobbing to her home.

Her mother took a different view. 'He's a holy old man, daughter. He can't have meant any harm. Go back and find out what was on his mind.'

Timidly the daughter returned, and asked the monk what he'd meant by his actions.

'It's too late,' he replied, 'just too late...'

'What do you mean?'

'Well, you see, as I was sitting here in meditation, I realized that the abbot of the local monastery had just died. And, uh, to put it bluntly, he'd not been a very good man. Quite corrupt, really. And, well, those asses in the field over there, they had started to copulate. Now some of that old abbot's karma was coming to fruition, and I saw that he was about to take re-birth as an ass. So in an attempt to create more favourable conditions for his re-birth, I jumped on you. But you fought me off and now.. well, it's just too late...'[5]

It's not the act that counts but the intention behind it.

Skilful acts, proceeding from helpful, generous and wise intentions, undermine egocentricity, conduce to a sense of confident, energetic expansiveness and lead towards Enlightenment. Unskilful acts, proceeding from hateful or selfish intentions, reinforce egocentricity, give rise to constricted states of painful isolation and lead away from Enlightenment. Acts are skilful or unskilful depending upon whether they lead towards or away from Enlightenment.

Unlike many forms of theological ethics, the psychological ethics of Buddhism doesn't set about the task of human socialization by generating an irrational sense of guilt. So many people in Western society suffer from irrational guilt — a generalized sense of not being up to scratch, of not being worthy, of always having to prove oneself or to hide one or another aspect of oneself, because somewhere, somehow, one is stained and unclean.

Buddhist ethics, by contrast, appeals to our rational self-interest. Skilful acts naturally lead to happiness, unskilful one's to pain, the choice is ours. One of the most valuable things that Buddhism has to offer the modern West is a viable, functioning, guilt-free ethics. It sounds too good to be true. A dream diet: 'Eat as much as you like of whatever you like — weight loss guaranteed.' But it's not that simple, for although Buddhist ethics may eschew guilt, it doesn't dispense with the need for care and discipline. Moral conduct is something which one needs to train in.

The very idea of moral training comes to many of us in the West today freighted with a baggage of life-denying rigidity and dustiness. We find it hard to conceive of such a thing without some kind of negative association, be it militarism, dour Calvinism, rigid Orthodox Judaism, repressive Catholicism or Victorian Puritanism. But it need not be so. From a Buddhist perspective, the greater one's level of ethical acuity, the more joyful and harmonious one's interaction with other living beings. The goal of Buddhist ethical training is the dissolution of the barrier between oneself and others. This is a result which accrues, not at some distant point in the future, but as the immediate consequence of adopting more skilful mental states. Ethical skilfulness leads to happiness and confidence. One of the characteristics which I've noticed marks out my Buddhist friends from others in our culture is just that — they are happier.

Over the centuries Buddhism has generated a variety of codes for ethical conduct. These are not regarded as commandments, but rather as 'training principles'. They are one of the ways in which Buddhists put the act of Going for Refuge to the Three Jewels into effect in their daily lives. By trying to act more and more skilfully one increasingly orients oneself towards the values which are embodied in the Buddha, the Dharma and the Sangha — the transcendental truth of non-selfhood; those acts of body, speech and mind which conduce towards selflessness; and the community of men and women whose behaviour is fundamentally unselfish and therefore always spontaneously altruistic.

The most common formulation of a Buddhist ethical code is the list of Five Precepts, which are followed in many parts of the Buddhist world.

I undertake not to kill.

I undertake not to take what has not been given.

I undertake not to engage in sexual misconduct.

I undertake not to lie.

I undertake to avoid intoxicants.

The precepts are intended as a support to spiritual training, a way of helping people to transform every dimension of their lives: their body, speech and mind. This is brought out more clearly in the following 'positive' formulation.

With deeds of loving kindness, I purify my body.

With open-handed generosity, I purify my body.

With stillness, simplicity and contentment, I purify my body.

With truthful communication, I purify my speech.

With mindfulness, clear and radiant, I purify my mind.[6]

Kindness, generosity, contentment, honesty and clarity —
these are markers along a path of practice which is constantly
oriented towards self-transcendence.

*I undertake not to kill. With deeds of loving kindness, I purify
my body.*

To kill another is the ultimate act of dualism. It is the epit-
ome of the subject/object divide for it requires the suspen-
sion, for a time at least, of that empathy with living beings to
which Buddhists aspire.

*First he will diligently foster the thought that his fellow creatures
are the same as himself. 'All have the same sorrows, the same
joys as I, and I must guard them like myself ... I will cease to live
as self and take as myself my fellow-creatures.'*

*We love our hands and other limbs, as members of the body;
then why not love other living beings as members of the
universe? By constant use man comes to imagine that his body,
which has no self-being, is a 'self'; then why should he not
conceive his 'self' to lie in his fellows also? ... Then, as you
would guard yourself against suffering and sorrow, so exercise
the spirit of helpfulness and tenderness to the world.*[7]

If you feel a pain in your foot your hand doesn't stay there,
safely out of the way, thinking 'I'm the hand. That pain is
the foot's problem. I'm not in pain. I'll just stay up here,
where it's safe.' No, as soon as you feel a pain in the foot the
hand reaches down to soothe the foot. Just so would we
respond to other living beings were we more continually

aware of the reality of the inter-connectedness of all living things.

The isolated egocentricity which leads us to value ourselves more than others, even to the point of being willing to destroy them, is the source of all suffering. By practising kindness and care for others the attachments of egocentricity are undermined and gradually begin to give way to an empathetic awareness of other people and other forms of life.

Unlike the Judaeo-Christian ethical system, where man has sole dominion over other living beings, Buddhism values the life of all sentient beings and many Buddhists therefore practise both pacifism and vegetarianism. This is not to say that such practices are universally enjoined by Buddhism. They are not. Some Buddhist scriptures and teachers enjoin them, others are more ambivalent. In the end each Buddhist will have to make up his or her own mind in these matters depending upon the conditions within which they find themselves. One can never assert that any act is skilful or unskilful in all times and in all places. The principle of conditionality applies within the arena of ethics as much as it does anywhere else. But to willingly take the life of another sentient being is a very serious matter indeed.

It is one thing to proclaim the ideal of loving others as much as oneself, another thing to practise it. But Buddhism doesn't just proclaim the ideal and leave us to get on with it. As we shall see in the section on meditation, it also offers a number of effective spiritual practices whose purpose is to help one to change oneself: to become less self-oriented, more open and expansive.

Ethics, meditation and reflection stand in an augmentative relationship to one another. Through meditation and reflection one can begin to change one's basic volitions, replacing selfish volitions with kindly ones. By acting out of kinder volitions one strengthens them and, in dependence upon the expansiveness which follows from acts of kindness, one's meditation and reflection go deeper.

I undertake not to take what has not been given. With open-handed generosity, I purify my body.

We live in a world of limited material resources whose dominant political ideology is premised upon the overriding benefits of universal material consumption. Environmentalists and social reformers blame politicians for their apparent lack of political will to address the fundamental problems of environmental despoliation and the relative inequity of wealth. But how much can politicians really do? Although they may occasionally have the power to ameliorate some of the problems which result from consumerism, the root causes of it run deeper than politics can reach. The fundamental drive towards consumption is intrinsic to the state of un-Enlightenment. To be is to consume.

Our real material needs are very simple: food, shelter, clothing and medicine. But, from the limited store of the world's resources, we take a great deal more than that. Western society is based, in large part, upon the neurotic urge to over-consumption. We consume in order to assert the fact of our existence. What we have, what we own, defines us in relation to others: the address we live at, the food we eat, the clothes we wear, the car we drive — we commit enormous amounts of energy to maintaining a fragile sense of identity in the face of change and emptiness.

This fundamental tendency to appropriation can be undermined by the conscious cultivation of the practice of generosity.

There is a generalized prejudice in the West today against the conscious cultivation of positive virtues. To do so seems somehow inauthentic and we tend to associate it with forced smiles and tedious do-good-ism. But consciously cultivating skilful mental states is not the same as rigidly repressing one's true urges and pretending to feel otherwise. You can only change yourself for the better by first acknowledging how you really are and what you really feel. But how we are and what we feel can be changed through the sensitive application of intelligent, conscious effort.

We all, for example, have experienced the arising of momentary generous impulses — 'I should give my friend a copy of that book, she'd really enjoy it.' But we don't act, time passes and the impulse fades away. By consciously resolving to act on one's generous impulses, however, one begins to act on at least a few of them. The resulting positive consequences — a sense of freedom and expansiveness — strengthen such impulses in the future. In time, the practice of generosity can become habitual.

I undertake not to engage in sexual misconduct. With stillness, simplicity and contentment, I purify my body.

The sense of generalized guilt which one finds in the West affects many of us across the whole spectrum of our lives. But in most people it finds its most acute expression in the area of sexual behaviour. Many Westerners, even today, feel furtive and shameful about this area of basic human behaviour.

Sexual behaviour has been singled out within Western culture for very particular attention. So much is this the case, in fact, that nowadays when one speaks of 'morality' many people take one to mean sexual morality. This is not the case in Buddhism, which has a much more straightforward approach to questions of sexuality. There is no reason, in principle, why Buddhists should not be heterosexual, homosexual, onanistic, transvestite or celibate, or why they should not practise monogamy, serial monogamy, polygamy, polyandry or, within limits, promiscuity.

This is not to underestimate the strength of sexual desire, nor to underrate its potential destructiveness. Indeed, the Buddha himself said that were there any other desire as strong as that of man for woman the spiritual life would be impossible. Craving, which often most acutely manifests as sexual craving, is the root cause of suffering. We are never so acutely separated from the rest of life as we are when in states of intense, frustrated sexual desire. Nonetheless, sexuality is no cause for guilt. We are subject to sexual desire just as we are subject to all kinds of other desires: we want food, shelter, praise, comfort and wealth as well. Desires can be healthy (we need food when we are hungry) or neurotic (we want food when we're depressed). In the same way there is an ordinary, healthy, human level of sexual desire and there is neurotic sexual craving, where we try to use the intense pleasure of sex to blot out our sense of existential anxiety. The task of overcoming neurotic desire, of transforming the cravings which keep one bound to the Wheel into the powerful desire for reality which helps one to move towards the horizon, is hindered, not helped, by feelings of irrational guilt about our ordinary human functions.

Western culture has long romanticized coupledom. Monogamous, heterosexual relationships are sanctified by the

Church and eulogised in literature and popular culture. Buddhism, by contrast, has never ennobled the nuclear couple. Marriage is not a sacrament in Buddhism — it is simply a social contract — and if one looks at the various Buddhist cultures around the world one finds socially accepted instances of monogamy, polygamy and polyandry. These are just different ways of arranging one's life. Whatever one's sexual preferences, the important thing is not to harm oneself or others by one's sexual behaviour.

And one should not place too much emphasis on the value of sex itself. It is at the centre of so many people's lives. I used to notice, when I travelled in Asia, the refreshing absence of a certain tension in the air. It took me a little while to realize what this was, but then I saw: I was not constantly being bombarded with overt sexual imagery. Unfortunately, with increasing Westernisation, this is beginning to change now, for Western culture places a hugely disproportionate emphasis on sex. We see it everywhere: in newspapers, magazines, books, films and television.

In practising Buddhism, one begins to get sex into proportion. One doesn't allow it to dominate the whole of one's life.

I undertake not to lie. With truthful communication, I purify my speech.

All human relationships are based upon communication. Society, culture, and social stability — all these depend upon the truth. If we can't have faith that what is being communicated is, in an ordinary sense, true, then society rapidly breaks down. To lie is to undermine the very foundation of human interaction.

To lie is also to diminish yourself, for in most cases we do so in order to protect our ego-identity. In lying, we take refuge in self-protectiveness, thus preserving a narrow, confining sphere of self-preoccupation.

Untruthfulness goes against the whole intention of the Buddhist spiritual life. By perpetuating delusions it preserves the fog of unreality.

> *If you speak delusions, everything becomes a delusion;*
> *If you speak the truth, everything becomes the truth.*
> *Outside the truth there is no delusion,*
> *But outside delusion there is no special truth.*
> *Followers of the Buddha's Way!*
> *Why do you earnestly seek the truth in distant places?*
> *Look for delusion and truth in the bottom of your own hearts.*[8]

We live in a world which takes untruth very lightly. We expect not to hear the truth from politicians, we know that advertisers are selective in the facts they bring to our attention and we take it for granted that what they say is hyperbolic (to say the least). Truth has given way to 'public relations', in a world where image is more important than fact.

This is morally and spiritually corrosive and leads to superficiality. The devaluation of simple truthfulness is one of the most pressing issues facing the world today. In response to this, one of the most important things one can do is to try to discover and proclaim the truth in any situation.

I undertake to avoid intoxicants. With mindfulness, clear and radiant, I purify my mind.

Buddhism has no puritanical objection to the reasonable use of alcohol. Nor does it single drink out as the main means of intoxication. Shopping, television, overwork, gambling, chocolate, compulsive altruism, sex, drink and drugs: all these can be used to numb the mind and dull the pain and anxieties of life. But they also lead to a diminution of life itself.

Buddhism is not against joy and pleasure. But it suggests that the dulled state of intoxication is actually *un*pleasant and we only choose to enter into it because it seems to offer some temporary respite from the pain of ordinary existence. Instead of trying to just blot out the pain of our daily lives, Buddhism suggests that we can consciously cultivate states which are not painful. A clear mind, aesthetic appreciation, the love of nature, meditation, kindness and friendship — all of these bring about skilful mental states, in dependence on which ever greater joy arises.

Like all other positive mental states, the clarity of mind which Buddhist ethics enjoins can be consciously cultivated. One of the most direct means of doing so is through the practice of meditation.

---

1. Friedrich Nietzsche, *The Gay Science*, transl. Kaufman, Vintage, 1974.

2. Exodus ch.20, v.1.

3. *Akusala.*

4. From the *Sutta Nipata*, transl. Dharmachari Vipassi, unpublished.

5. It's important to 'read' this story from a Tibetan perspective, by the way. It assumes that the girl would have been delighted to have been the mother of a re-incarnated abbot!

6. *The FWBO Puja Book*, Windhorse Publications, Birmingham, 1966.

7. L.D. Barnett, *The Path of Light*, rendered from *The Bodhicharyavatara of Santideva*, reprinted London 1959.

8. *One Robe, One Bowl: the Zen Poetry of Ryokan*, transl. John Stevens, Weatherhill, 1977.

Chapter 6

Meditation and Ritual

By the time of the Buddha, the tradition of meditation practice was well established in Asia, and although the Buddha
himself took the practice to new heights, he did not invent it.
Rather, he was instructed in it by his own teachers, two of
whom, Alara Kalama and Udraka Ramaputra, we read about
in the scriptures. Behind these figures the lineages of meditation instruction disappear backwards into the mists of time.
They are the earliest documented teachers of meditation, and
although we don't know who their teachers were, we do
know that the South Asian religious traditions of their time
were very familiar with the arts of contemplative introspection and that those arts, exported throughout the Asian world,
have continued to be cultivated in lineages of practice right
up to the present day.

Although the tradition of systematic meditation has a long
history in the East, it is only very recently that the Western
religious traditions have begun to notice its significance more
widely. In 1989, for example, Pope John Paul II approved and
ordered the publication of a *Letter to the Bishops of the Catholic
Church on Some Aspects of Christian Meditation* which had
been drawn up by the Congregation for the Doctrine of the
Faith (the modern successor of the Inquisition) and signed by
Cardinal Ratzinger. The letter begins:

*Many Christians today have a keen desire to learn how to experi-
ence a deeper and authentic prayer life despite the not*

inconsiderable difficulties which modern culture places in the way of the need for silence, recollection and meditation. The interest which in recent years has been awakened also among some Christians by forms of meditation associated with some eastern religions and their particular methods of prayer is a significant sign of this need for spiritual recollection and a deep contact with the divine mystery...

The letter goes on to consider the theological and spiritual implications of issues arising for Catholics from the growing interest in 'eastern methods' of meditation. In seeking to clarify matters, the Cardinal sets out to draw distinctions:

With the present diffusion of eastern methods of meditation in the Christian world and in ecclesiastical communities, we find ourselves faced with the pointed renewal of an attempt which is not free from dangers and errors, to fuse Christian meditation with that which is non-Christian. ... [Some] do not hesitate to place that absolute without image or concepts, which is proper to Buddhist theory, on the same level as the majesty of God revealed in Christ, which towers above finite reality. ... These and similar proposals to harmonize Christian meditation with eastern techniques need to have their contents and methods ever subjected to a thorough-going examination so as to avoid the danger of falling into syncretism.

Three points emerge here which are relevant to the subject of Buddhist meditation as practised in the West.

Firstly, the letter is, in itself, an indicator of the growing interest being shown, throughout our society, in Buddhist and other 'eastern' meditation techniques. When the modern successor to the Inquisition speaks out, something interesting must be happening. The letter is also an indicator of the extent to which people in our society seem to feel the need (which, for them, orthodox Christian teaching appears not to have addressed) for a means whereby they can return to themselves and discover their own deeper 'interiority'. Finally, the letter points to a tendency for techniques such as meditation to be treated as intrinsically separable from their Buddhist and other eastern religious contexts.

The root cause of the growing contemporary Western interest in meditation is no different from the interest in it which has been shown at any other time or place. It is founded in a single common experience – 'My life is not what it could be. Things could be better.' For some this manifests as a religious or existential quest: 'What is the real meaning of life? What is the ultimate truth of things?' Others just want to learn to concentrate more effectively, or to relax more deeply. Some come to meditation on the basis of medical referrals (and there is a growing tendency amongst doctors to 'prescribe' meditation), others because it has seemed to make their friends happier and more effective. But whatever their reasons for wanting to learn meditation may be, for the past thirty years or so increasing numbers of Westerners have been drawn to the practice.

Meditation began to be widely popularized in the West when the Beatles set out for India on a well-publicized spiritual quest which culminated in their meeting the Maharishi Mahesh Yogi. The Maharishi (today known as His Holiness Maharishi Mahesh Yogi) in turn came to the West and the Transcendental Meditation (TM) technique which he brought with him, enthusiastically taken up and vigorously marketed by his followers, played a large part in making meditation a household word in the West today.

The TM movement makes extravagant claims for its programme of meditation. Claims which, it asserts, are all scientifically verified.

... For example, the finding that the Transcendental Meditation and TM-Sidhi (sic) program decreases stress is validated by physiological changes such as decreased ... muscle tension, normalization of blood pressure, increased autonomic stability, and increased EEG coherence ... Likewise, stress reduction is demonstrated by the sociological changes, such as decreased hostility, increased family harmony, and reduced criminal behaviour in incarcerated felons. Moreover, research extends the concept of stress reduction to the ecological level. Studies have found that the reduction of stress in meditating individuals creates an influence of harmony in the environment. Scientists have named this phenomenon the Maharishi Effect — *the finding that even one per cent of the population practising the Transcendental Meditation technique, or the square root of one percent practising the more advanced Transcendental Meditation-Sidhi program, improves the quality of life, as indicated by such changes as reduced crime and sickness in the larger society.*[1]

These 'scientific' findings are a matter of some dispute:

Frankly, the reported effects of TM upon human behaviour are trivial. Considering the alleged potency of the TM procedure, the changes in physiological and behavioural measures are conspicuously minute. It is only within the context of certain testing procedures that small changes become exaggerated out of proportion. People are overcome frequently by numbers and no doubt the systematic analyses of data can be boring. However, the TM movement has played heavily upon this format. Like a madman who goes about measuring everything in his path in order to prove that objects have length, avid TMers have used the scientific method.[2]

Whatever one makes of the TM preoccupation with data, there is no doubt that the Maharishi and his followers played a large part in making the practice of meditation seem less strange and exotic in the West today. At beginners' meditation classes these days one meets people from all walks of life — students, housewives, policemen, doctors, lawyers, bricklayers, artists — and generally speaking, for the large majority of these, the idea of taking up the practice of meditation is something quite simple and straightforward. It is not thought of as exotic or in any way peculiar, it is not something which one wouldn't talk about to one's friends. When Sangharakshita returned to the West in 1964 he was told by one British Buddhist luminary that English people shouldn't be expected to meditate for more than five minutes at a time, for meditation was thought of as quite dangerous and rather exotic.

How things have changed in the last thirty years. Today, in almost every town or city in the Western hemisphere one can go along and attend a course or class where the fundamental bases of meditation will be taught by reasonably experienced meditation teachers; usually Buddhist, but occasionally from the Hindu tradition as well. Meditation has become very popular indeed.

There are hundreds, possibly thousands, of different meditation techniques which have evolved over the last few thousand years in the East and all of these will be effective to some extent — once one sits down and begins to work directly upon the mind, changes in one's mental state begin to occur. But different techniques bring about different changes. Not all changes are equally desirable (some aren't desirable at all), and some changes can only effectively take place upon previously established foundations. The practice of meditation needs to be approached systematically. This is not a point which is fully appreciated by all those who teach meditation and, although it is generally far better to learn the practice from an experienced meditation instructor rather than from a book, it is very much a case of *caveat emptor* — let the buyer beware — not all meditations are equally effective and not all instructors are equally able.

Different meditation practices will be appropriate at different times and under different conditions and, within the emerging Western Buddhist traditions, the range of available practices is very large. Surveying the different types of meditation which are practised within the Buddhist tradition as a whole, one can divide them into five broad categories. Although not used equally by all the traditions, each of these practices can have its place within the spiritual life of the individual meditator.

The simplest and most fundamental meditation practices are those which are designed to generate and enhance concentration. After these come practices whose purpose is to cultivate emotional positivity of one kind or another. Then there are 'formless' practices whose purpose is to encourage the process of letting go of attachments. Allied to these, but taking a different approach, are practices whose purpose is the direct development of spiritual insight. Finally, there are visualization practices which engage with archetypal representations of transcendental experience. I will describe examples of each of these below.

Although these five types of practice are all very different, they stand in close relation to one another and are, in an important sense, 'holographic' — all the elements of any one practice are ultimately contained in all the others. One cannot visualize, for example, without some degree of concentration, but the attempt to visualize also develops concentration. One cannot 'let go' without some degree of emotional positivity, but one cannot really develop emotional positivity unless one can, to some extent at least, let go of negativity. In this way all of these practices stand in mutually augmentative relationship to one another.

That said, one can nonetheless discern a kind of hierarchy, or system of practice. Some practices are generally better taken up before others, and this systemization can be related to the levels of Going for Refuge. Generally speaking, those practices which develop concentration and positive emotion are suited to the provisional level of Going for Refuge. The last two kinds of practice — insight practices and archetypal visualisation — are more existentially challenging and should only be taken up by those who are ready to make a significant spiritual commitment to practice, at the level of effective Going for Refuge. Formless meditations, depending on the way in which they are taught, bridge the two levels.

The most common forms of meditation are those whose purpose is to develop concentration. In this type of practice you select an object of concentration and try to keep your attention undistractedly upon it for a period of time. All kinds of objects can be used: a candle flame, a brightly coloured disk, a geometric pattern, a pebble, a mantra or a sound. But one of the most common objects is the breath. The mindfulness of breathing practice, which I will describe below, helps to bring about higher levels of mental focus, concentration and integration.

We live in an increasingly non-physical world with a great deal of mental distraction. In consequence people in our society are often mentally hyperactive and mentally fragmented. With so much stimulation about one's attention is pulled now this way, now that. According to educational psychologists,

the average attention span amongst children is rapidly diminishing. Amongst adults it's not that high. But the psychic fragmentation one so often finds in the West has deeper roots.
We are also split between our conscious and our unconscious
minds. The process of socialization we undergo goes hand in
hand with one or another kind of repression. We learn to
repress unacceptable feelings, thoughts and desires in order
to fit in, to be acceptable and to find our place in the world.
But what is repressed doesn't just conveniently vanish and,
so long as we remain unaware of it, tends to return to
consciousness in ways which afflict our conscious behaviour.
More consciously perhaps, we are also split between conflicting desires — we want to eat that chocolate but we want to
remain slim; we want the comfort of that sexual relationship
but we want to be free.

The mindfulness of breathing practice is designed to address
the issue of psychic fragmentation. Like all of the practices I
will describe here, it is taken up in one or another standard
meditation posture, such as one would learn at most meditation classes. I am not trying to teach meditation here. That is
best done face to face by a meditation instructor. Nonetheless,
I will describe a few of the more common practices in some
detail to give at least the beginnings of an idea of what meditation is all about.

The mindfulness of breathing practice is divided into four
stages of more or less equal length. Most people begin by
sitting for between ten and twenty minutes. More experienced meditators usually sit for between forty minutes and
an hour, but there is no rule about this.

The idea behind the mindfulness of breathing is that one
simply brings one's attention to bear upon the process of
breathing, attending ever more closely to the process itself.

You don't try to adjust the breath in any way. You don't try to breathe more deeply or more slowly, but just follow the natural course of the breath as it occurs. In the first stage, you breathe in, breathe out, and (sub-vocally) count 'one'. Breathe in, breathe out, count 'two', and so on up to ten, after which you simply repeat the cycle again — counting to yourself after each out-breath.

The second stage follows the same procedure, but with the slight additional subtlety that in this stage you count before the in-breath rather than after the out-breath. You anticipate the breath which is about to come. So you count 'one', breathe in, breathe out. Count 'two', breathe in, breathe out. And so on up to ten and then returning to one, count the breaths, from one to ten, over and over.

In the third stage you stop counting and just follow the breath, attending closely to it as it enters your nose, passes down your throat, fills your lungs, passes back up your throat and leaves your body. Your diaphragm moves up and down, your chest expands and contracts. Every moment of attention yields more and more subtlety, for the breath is a truly marvellous phenomenon and breathing can be a deeply pleasing aesthetic act. Like waves breaking on a calm beach, each breath is different, each has its own uniquely detailed form and beauty.

In the fourth stage you bring your attention to bear on that single point where the breath first enters your body — often as a slight tickle at the tip of your nostrils. However it presents itself, this is a fine, subtle sensation. Attending one-pointedly to that sensation one can experience very high levels of calm concentration.

In the Mindfulness of Breathing, as in all the forms of meditation I will discuss here, you never try to force your mind to attend. That is always counter-productive, like trying to smooth water with an iron. Rather, you allow your attention to gather and settle, coaxing your mind with a steady effort. Very few people find meditation naturally easy. When I first sat down to meditate I was astonished to see how un-calm my mind was. Like a hyperactive monkey in a cage, it rushed now here, now there; grasping onto this thought, clinging onto that. Never settling for more than a moment. All that frenetic, pointless, undirected activity. I wonder that I ever managed to get anything done at all. There are a number of hindrances to the process of meditation and tradition has developed a number of antidotes to the hindrances. Again, one can learn these at a meditation class, and it is worth making the effort to do so, for the experience of the mind settled in meditation is one of the most deeply pleasing, deeply integrating experiences available.

The *experience* of integration, strangely enough, has deep philosophical implications.

...From Descartes on, the guiding question in Western philosophy has been whether body and mind are one or two substances ... and what the ontological relation between them is. We have already seen the simple, experiential, pragmatic approach taken in mindfulness/awareness meditation. It is a matter of simple experience that our mind and body can be dissociated, that the mind can wander, that we can be unaware of where we are and what our mind and body are doing. But this situation, this habit of mindlessness, can be changed. Body and mind can be brought together. We can develop habits in which body and mind are fully coordinated. The result is a mastery that is not only known to the individual meditator himself but that is visible to others — we easily recognize by its precision and grace a gesture that is

*animated by full awareness. We typically associate such mindful-
ness with the actions of an expert such as an athlete or musician.*

*...Descartes' conclusion that he was a thinking thing [cogito ergo
sum — I think, therefore I am] was the product of his question,
and that question was the product of specific practices — those of
disembodied, unmindful reflection... And although it has recently
become fashionable to criticize or 'deconstruct' this standpoint of
the cogito, philosophers still do not depart from the basic practice
responsible for it.*[3]

The forms of introspection which have, to date, been available to Western philosophers as the raw material of their
craft, have been very limited in their scope and have consequently produced limited world-views. Western culture's
relative lack of 'interiority' plays its part in other realms as
well. It has had a huge impact on the arts and it is one of the
central determinants in late twentieth century culture, so
much marked by stress, superficiality and materialism.
Without being unduly utopian, we can nevertheless imagine
that as the techniques of meditation come to be more widely
practised in the West significant social changes may follow.

Although Buddhism is often thought of as generally negative
and pessimistic, the Abhidharma tradition of scholastic analysis, which set out to categorize all possible mental events,
discerned far more that were positive than negative. Mental
states, in Buddhism, are never thought of as merely 'given'.
All mental states arise in dependence upon conditions and by
changing the conditions which give rise to negative mental
states you can replace them with more positive ones.

Using the Brahminical terminology of his times, but giving it
a unique twist, the Buddha redefined the idea of a 'Heavenly

state'[4]. There are four sublime states, he taught, but they aren't 'heavens' in the sense of being a more or less physical location, elsewhere. Rather they are the states of loving kindness, compassion, sympathetic joy and equanimity[5]. Each of these states can be consciously cultivated, and the tradition has developed specific practices for the development of each. I will describe one of these below.

The Pali word *metta* is sometimes translated as 'loving-kindness', and that is perhaps the best we can do with it. But it isn't really satisfactory. It would be easier to use just 'love', but that word has been so much debased in English: you can love ice-cream, your parents, your favourite pullover, your lover, your dog and the most recent pop star. 'Love' often has connotations of sentiment and craving which are inappropriate here. *Metta* means something more like 'universal loving-kindness'. Quite a mouthful. Perhaps it's better to leave it untranslated and hope that, like the word *karma*, it will eventually just enter our language.

Bhavana means something like 'cultivation', so the *metta bhavana* practice is concerned with the cultivation of universal loving kindness. All the major religions seem to agree that loving-kindness is a good thing. But few of them give their followers any idea of how to cultivate it. In the Judaeo-Christian tradition, indeed (with stories like that of Job), one is left with a sense that perhaps the best thing one can do about one's states of mind is simply learn to endure them. The quality of endurance is no bad thing, but Buddhism would also suggest that one can learn to change one's mental states appreciably for the better. Lacking the sense that 'we are as we are because we are as God made us', Buddhism emphasizes the constant possibility of changing one's mental state for the better and it teaches a number of techniques to bring such changes about. The *metta bhavana* practice is one of these.

The practice is divided into five stages of more or less equal length. In it, you set out to cultivate feelings of warmth, kindness, goodwill — *metta* — first of all towards yourself; then to a close friend; to a neutral person; an enemy; and finally to all beings everywhere.

You begin with yourself because, as the old adage goes, if you can't love yourself you can't love others. A common psychological characteristic of people living in the West today is a sense of low self-esteem. There are many reasons for this: the extensive use of guilt as a means of control in the Judaeo-Christian tradition; the breakdown of family and other relationships; rootlessness; heightened social mobility (which leads to exaggerated personal expectations); and those social dogmas which demonize men and promise women the skies — all of these contribute to a pervading sense that one is somehow not up to the mark, not good enough, never quite adequate.

It has been very sobering, over the years that I've taught this practice, to see how many people struggle with the first stage. For many it comes as something of a revelation — they sit down to cultivate feelings of warmth and kindness towards themselves and then discover that they don't really like themselves very much at all. But perseverance furthers and technique helps. A good teacher will be able to suggest a number of ways in which you can begin to work with and change your feelings at this stage of the practice.

Next you call to mind a close friend (not someone to whom you're sexually attracted; not your parent or child; and someone who is currently alive: one shouldn't confuse *metta* with other strong emotions) and you set about cultivating feelings of *metta* towards your friend.

Then you bring to mind someone you see quite often but to whom you have no strong feelings one way or another, and you cultivate *metta* towards them.

Then you recollect an enemy, or someone with whom your communication may be a bit rough or brittle, and you culti-vate *metta* towards them. After all, they are human too. They want to find happiness, they want to avoid pain. They may not be going about it very effectively (who knows?), but their desires are ultimately not that different from your own. At all of these stages there are a number of techniques you can use to help you to develop real feelings of warmth and goodwill. For you are not trying here just to think well of someone. That is a start, but it is only a start. The goal of the practice is to change the way you feel — the way you *really* feel — in your heart.

In the fifth and final stage you bring to mind all four people — yourself, your friend, the neutral person and the enemy — and you try to feel *metta* for all four persons equally. If you were all four in a hot-air balloon which was about to crash and one of you had to jump out to lighten the load you would not know who to choose. Then you begin to radiate the feel-ing of *metta* outwards: to all the people in the building you're in; all the people in the neighbourhood; the town; the state; the continent — to all living beings in all directions of space...

Doing the practice actually changes how you feel, even if it can be something of a struggle sometimes. Doing it regularly, over a number of years, you begin to develop a reservoir of *metta* which you can draw on more or less at will. The *metta bhavana* practice is powerfully transforming.

To practise meditation is to encounter the open dimension of being. For you come to the practice in one state of mind, a state which may seem fixed, final and all pervading, and you leave the practice in another state of mind. It is as if, over the course of the practice, you pass from one world into another, and that passage, to whatever extent it takes place, is by way of the open dimension.

The mindfulness of breathing and the *metta bhavana* are both quite highly structured practices and, given the extent of mental and emotional fragmentation that modern life produces, most of us need such structures as the fundamental basis of our practice. But over the centuries the Buddhist tradition also generated a number of unstructured, or 'formless' meditations. The Japanese Zen practice of *zazen* (which translates as 'meditation'), the Tibetan practices of *mahamudra*[6] and *dzogchen*[7] are all instances of these. In these practices one simply sits, in the open dimension. That is all.

The modern Western tendency, which reacts to practice and discipline and upholds a kind of sloppy spontaneity, might find these practices quite attractive at first. At first. One should never underestimate the kind of discipline which is needed to just sit, with your own mind, for a fixed period, day, after day, after day.

Another approach to the open dimension is by way of direct, cognitive contemplation. This is not the same as discursive thinking, rather it is an attempt to allow the truths of the Dharma to penetrate more deeply into the psyche and to allow your frame of reference, the cognitive underpinning of your entire state of being, to be directly changed by it. This is done by way of 'insight' practice. There are any number of these in the tradition, but they generally proceed in more or less the same way. You begin by establishing mindfulness and positive emotion. These practices can be existentially shocking and you need a high level of positivity to absorb the shock. In the absence of such positivity the open dimension might appear as the shadow form of spiritual creativity — solipsistic nihilism.

Having established mindfulness and positivity, you select an object of contemplation. You might contemplate 'not-self'. Whatever occurs, you note that it is not yourself. Thoughts which arise and pass away are not yourself. Feelings, sensations, impulses — all these simply arise in the mind and pass away. None of them is the self; they are all simply transitory, fleeting phenomena; they come into the mind and pass out of it. The body is not the self — it is just a changing collection of cells and chemicals; feelings and sensations. Contemplating like this for a time, noting the arising and passing away of phenomena, you see that the mind is not the self either — for where is the mind? What are its boundaries? What is its form? The idea of the self is just an idea. Like everything else it arises, changes and passes away. The intention of such practices is to liberate the mind. To set it free from the prison of mental constructs. But what is the nature of the mind thus liberated? That cannot be said, it can only be known in direct experience.

Finally, we come to those kinds of meditation practice which engage with archetypal representations of transcendental experience by way of visualization practice.

Systematically engaging with meditation practice, one begins to see that there is a kind of hierarchy of mental states. People often come to the practice with minds that are quite fragmented. The first thing they need to do is to develop at least the rudimentary beginnings of a kind of workable selfhood. By this I just mean some kind of coherent sense of a more or less singular personality – which knows at least to some extent what it wants, thinks and feels; which is reasonably integrated; and in which all the various sub-personalities are willing, more or less, to cooperate upon a common project.

In the process of developing this rudimentary level of integration, by way of meditation, communication, ethical conduct and other spiritual practices, you come to notice that different mental states have very different qualities. Some are very egocentred. Strong craving, for example, or animosity, draws you in around yourself into a hard knot of egocentricity. Concern for others, or the calm, un-self-concerned appreciation of natural beauty, leads to mental states which are broader and finer — more expansive, less ego-oriented. In this way you can begin to discern a hierarchy of mental states that starts with crude self-preoccupation, distracted fragmentation and dissipation, and ascends by degrees of refinement and integration towards higher and ever higher levels of finesse, strength, energy, subtlety, insight and selflessness. There is no limit at the top of this hierarchy. No end to refinement, where the universe, as it were, says 'Stop! This far and no further!' There is only the horizon of the known, beyond which lie dimensions of being and consciousness about which we can, by definition, say nothing at all.

We live and practise very much on this side of the horizon, but one of the ways in which we can engage with what lies over the horizon is by means of the imagination. For, looked at with the eye of the imagination, one can see, reflected in the sky above the horizon, images and reflections of transcendental reality, archetypal manifestations which are produced by the interaction between the imagination and transcendental reality.

Over the years the various different qualities of the Enlightened mind have presented themselves to experienced meditators in the form of subtle, translucent embodiments. Human, divine or demonic in appearance, these all represent one or another aspect of Enlightened consciousness. There are a number of practices centred around the contemplation of these forms. Some are very complex, involving the visualization of hundreds of figures in great detail. Most are much simpler. One of these (highly simplified here) is the contemplation of the bodhisattva Tara—the quintessence of Enlightened compassion.

You begin by establishing mindfulness and *metta*, and then visualize a clear blue sky, luminous, unobstructed in all directions. This is the open dimension. Out of the sky, a large lotus flower appears—white, tinged with blue—and upon the calyx of the lotus is a glowing white mat, round like the moon, stainlessly pure. Upon this mat sits the bodhisattva Tara. She is made entirely of jade green light, translucent as a rainbow. Ornamented with fine silks and sparkling jewels, with full breasts and narrow waist, Tara protects all beings with the kindness of a mother. Her left leg is drawn up in meditation posture, whilst her right steps down into the world, stepping out to help living beings everywhere. Her left hand, gently grasping the stalk of a blue lotus flower that blooms above her shoulder, is held in a gesture which bestows fearlessness whilst her right arm is extended in the gesture of giving. Rainbow light streams outwards from her. Gathered up, it falls upon your own heart, conferring happiness and bliss.

Contemplating the figure for a time, you begin, sub-vocally, to recite her *mantra — om tare tuttare ture svaha —* over and over. Just as the figure of Tara is a symbol made of light, so the *mantra* is a symbol made of sound. Both of these symbols represent Tara herself, whose true essence can never be put into words.

After a time, all the forms dissolve back into the blue sky. The blue sky dissolves and the practice ends. Practices such as these belong to the tantric tradition and are most commonly found today in Tibetan Buddhism. To practise them effectively you need to be initiated into the practice in the context of a ceremony which establishes an effective link between you and the form which you are going to visualize. Such initiations should only be given to people who are effectively Going for Refuge, for the practice, to be effective, requires strong commitment and a firm basis.

As Buddhism comes to the West there is no doubt that, over time, the traditional forms will gradually become westernised. This is not a process which can be rushed; it will follow naturally from a deeper contact between Buddhism and the Western imagination in the context of profound meditation experience. Some Tibetan teachers recommend to their Western Buddhist students that they might choose to visualize Jesus or Mary instead of the traditional Buddhist forms. This approach ignores the deep differences in symbolic significance which exist between the Buddhist and Christian traditions. Jesus comes to Westerners carrying a huge burden of history. So much blood has been spilt in his name; so much guilt induced; so much enforced theology propounded. We approach figures like Tara with a clean slate. She may be iconographically strange to us, but she comes unburdened by history, free from repression and guilt. We must beware of giving this clarity away for the sake of a superficial cultural reconciliation.

In the Buddhist approach to spiritual life, meditation most often takes place in a ritual context. 'Superstition sets the whole world in flames; philosophy quenches them' wrote Voltaire in 1764 and, increasingly since the eighteenth century, the rational has overborne the irrational in Western cultural life. But the triumph of reason, Galileo's posthumous victory over the forces of dogmatic superstition, was founded upon a case of mistaken identity which has had grave consequences for Western psychological and spiritual life. For it is a profound mistake to identify what is merely irrational, contrary to logic and therefore mistaken, with what is non-rational or trans-rational — truths whose meaning cannot be expressed or bounded within the limits of reason alone.

Reason is crucially important but it reigns in just one of the many dimensions of human consciousness. A life based in reason alone would be arid beyond endurance. Kindness, love, beauty, adoration, empathy, compassion—none of these essential human experiences can be adequately accounted for in strictly logical terms. Nor can reason alone ever give an adequate account of what lies beyond the horizon of ordinary human consciousness. The closer one comes towards that horizon the more language based in reason gives way to languages based in myth and symbol. Poetic metaphors encompass far more than reasoned accounts.

They move us, shape our minds and transform our awareness, in ways reason cannot.

Unfortunately, we in the West today inherit a deep split between the faculties of thinking and feeling. Nowhere was this split more apparent than in the arena of pre-eighteenth century religious belief, where such faith and devotion as the common people felt was explicitly disconnected from any higher vision or insight. Theology was only ever the pursuit of a small elite. Instead of knowledge concerning religious matters there was only belief. Belief inevitably hardens into dogma and dogma in turn becomes irreconcilable with the intellect.[8] The eighteenth century rebellion against dogma, evidenced in figures like Voltaire, led to a deep suspicion of ritual and religion and perpetuated the split in new ways.

Reason and emotion come together in the imagination. 'Imagination' here is not the same as mere fantasy. It doesn't stand for that which isn't truly real. Just the opposite, in fact. To really see something — to see it in its very depths, as it really is — is to see it as marked with the characteristics of the open dimension.

All great art shows this to some extent. Van Gogh, for example, showed in his famous painting that a chair is not just a chair. It is a luminous, transitory phenomenon, alive with the marks of human creativity, significant far beyond its mere utility.

There are no 'things' in the open dimension, nothing which is fixed, final, stable — dead. All that there is is a fleeting, transitory succession of images. But images don't occur in isolation, intact and enclosed, cut-off from one another in little chunks of coherent finitude. Every image is fluid and changing, and it derives its meaning and significance from every other image. As I showed in the case of my *Lavatera Barnsley*, everything is interconnected in all dimensions.

To see things in their fullness is to see them as images, as symbols of reality. To truly see an image is to see into the open dimension.

...when one truly perceives an image one perceives it with the whole of oneself, or with one's whole being. When one truly perceives an image therefore, one is transported to the world where that image belongs and becomes, if only for the time being, an inhabitant of that world. In other words, truly to perceive an image means to become an image, so that when one speaks of the imagination, or the imaginal faculty, what one is really speaking of is image perceiving image.[9]

Buddhist rituals point to the open dimension. They do this in a number of ways but all have one thing in common — they are ways of engaging the imagination with the process of Going for Refuge. There are any number of different Buddhist rituals: from the relatively simple (bowing to images of the Buddha; making offerings to shrines) to the hugely elaborate and complex (Tibetan devotional cere-monies can last for several days). All of these are intended to bring about changes in the states of mind of the participants, to draw them closer to the horizon and to engage them more deeply in the world of the spiritual imagination.

The Westernization of Buddhist ritual is a gradual process. As we shall see in the next chapter, most Buddhist groups in the West have already gone a short way down this path. At the very least they have begun to translate a portion of their liturgies into the local language. Some organisations are engaged in ritual and liturgical experiment—chanting mantras in Western style three-part harmony, for example. Other experiments go a little further. The Friends of the Western Buddhist Order, for example, has begun to experi-ment with the relationship between ritual, drama, poetry and music.

In one such experiment, a group of Order members led a *Game of Life* retreat, where they tried to penetrate more deeply into the meaning of the traditional symbolism of the Wheel of Life by combining a conceptual exploration of that image with a living experience of it using the techniques of modern drama.

Participants on the retreat meditated together as usual, and engaged in the usual devotional ceremonies used in the FWBO, but they began the retreat by going though a set of 'warm-up' exercises such as are used in drama schools and before rehearsals by most theatre companies. Each day began with meditation and then there was a talk on one or another of the six realms of the Wheel of Life, drawing out the characteristics of each realm — its predominant emotional tone; the colours, images, mental states and other attributes associated with it. Those on retreat then brainstormed together, trying to draw out the different qualities of each realm, making their own particular (usually Western) imaginative connection with it. They then divided into two groups. One group made the realm using the plastic arts, lighting and so on, creating a kind of stage set in one part of the hall they were using. The other group set about trying to dramatise the experience of that realm using poetry, drama, costume, dance and music. In the evenings, both groups came together and a dramatic presentation of the realm took place in the world which had been created for it. The presentations, which were usually quite highly charged, always concluded with the devotional evocation of the particular Buddha form associated with that realm.

Each realm was left intact after the performance and by the end of the week the hall they were using had been transformed into a *mandala* of the six realms. These were then broken down, the materials were gathered together, and they then performed a devotional ceremony and ritually burned what they had made — returning everything to emptiness. Starting with a bare hall they ended with a bare hall. But in between, through the week, they had imaginatively traversed the six realms, engaging with them at a depth which, for all of the participants, had been unprecedented.

We have nothing like this any more in our culture, except perhaps a few surviving Passion Plays. The Greeks were keenly alive to the ritual nature of theatre, and this carried over to some extent into medieval times, but it is a tradition which we have sadly lost.

Some of the traditional Buddhist ritual forms, developed over hundreds of years in the countries of Asia, represent pinnacles of human artistic, psychological and spiritual endeavour. It will be many years before Western Buddhist forms achieve such heights. The experiments which the different Buddhist organisations are currently doing in this area, however, may one day be looked back upon as having been at the creative cutting edge of a Western spiritual and artistic renaissance.

---

1. *Summary of Scientific Research on the Transcendental Meditation and TM-Sidhi Program*, compiled and edited by David Orme-Johnson, Phd., published on the World Wide Web at http://www.miu.edu/TM_Research/Bibliographies/Research_Summaries.

2. M.A. Persinger, N. Carrey, and L. Suess, *TM and Cult Mania*, Christopher House Publishing, 1980.

3. Varela, Thompson and Rosch, *The Embodied Mind: Cognitive Science and Human Experience*, MIT Press, 1991.

4. *Brahma-vihara*.

5. Pali - *metta, karuna, mudita, upekkha*. Sanskrit – *maitri, karuna, mudita, upeksha*.

6. Sanskrit. Literally meaning "Great seal", *mahamudra* is taught by the Kagyu school of Tibetan Buddhism. Its essence is the effortless realization of the true nature of the mind.

7. Tibetan. Literally "Great Perfection". Practised in the Nyingma school of Tibetan Buddhism, is correlates closely with Mahamudra.

8. See Sanghrakshita, *Ritual and Devotion in Buddhism: an Introduction,* Windhorse Publications, 1995.

9. Sangharakshita, *The Priceless Jewel*, Windhorse Publications, 1993.

Chapter 7

Teachers, Students and Spiritual Friends

For the last two and a half thousand years, the essence of Buddhism has been chiefly preserved, not in books and philosophical treatises, but in lineages of spiritual transmission which are made up of personal relationships — links of care and concern between individual people.

Starting in the Deer Park at Sarnath, where the newly Enlightened Buddha met and engaged in discussion with those who were to form the beginnings of his new sangha, the teachings have been passed down through the ages in a vast enterprise of transmission consisting of innumerable personal relationships between teachers and disciples. Like an immense river network, such relationships have channelled a flow of spiritual friendship which began with the Buddha and which continues to live on today in the individual relationships between Buddhist teachers and their contemporary disciples.

Given the alienated, impersonal nature of Western culture, relationships of spiritual friendship are, perhaps, more important today than they have ever been before. We are used to receiving our information in highly impersonal ways and there is an enormous amount of information *about* Buddhism available today. We can read about it in books, see prog-rammes about it on television, hear lectures on it from academic specialists. But none of these, in themselves alone, can communicate its living essence.

That can only be transmitted by way of actual exemplifica-tion — by direct, face-to-face communication with a person who has at least some degree of spiritual insight. But the relationship between Buddhist teachers and their students has never, perhaps, been quite as problematic as it is in the West today.

The traditional, formalized, hierarchical relationship between teachers and students sits awkwardly with contem-porary Western views and presuppositions. On the one hand, it runs counter to the contemporary assumption of the absolute rectitude of egalitarianism. On the other, it becomes entangled with strong, unconscious impulses within the Western psyche that are brought about by a pervading sense of an absent father. Many Westerners feel a strong, unconscious need for a wise authority figure who will care for them and take responsibility for smoothing out all the messy contradictions in their lives.

Western Buddhists began to become conscious of the tension between these two positions only in the last decade or so. But it had been building up for some time. Buddhism came into the West along a particular cultural trajectory. Westerners heard about Buddhism long before any of them entered into one or another of the lineages of practice. It wasn't until the 1950s and 60s that significant numbers of Westerners actually began to engage with the Dharma existentially, and most of these came to Buddhism with their own very particular cultural agenda.

On the 9th of August 1945, an atomic bomb fell on Nagasaki, bringing World War II to an end and marking the beginning of the Nuclear Age. The Cold War which followed, with the threat of H-bombs and intercontinental ballistic missiles, was marked by high levels of semi-conscious dread and anxiety.

In America these came to a head in the McCarthy era: an intense period of paranoia and conformity, marked by a deep suspicion of all that was 'other'.

McCarthy-ism epitomized the repressive tendencies at work in 1950s America. The newly powerful industrial–military complex, buoyed by the Protestant work ethic and Cold War angst, brought about a culture of conformity in which good citizens marked their sense of belonging, and sought to drown their anxieties by embarking on a spree of consumerism. Never before in human history was so much available to so many. Chrome-plated tail-finned cars; ranch style suburban homes; barbecues and television — the new American Dream of a world of plenty, where democracy and technology would liberate mankind from the fearful shadow of Communism.

But the new consumerist conformity never quite managed to eradicate those other quintessential American daemons: the spirit of free enquiry; social and personal freedom; and the love of the open road. The shades of Henry Thoreau and Walt Whitman found new expression in the Beat Generation — Alan Ginsberg, Jack Kerouac, Gary Snyder and others gave voice to horrified protest as American society blindly embraced consumerism and corporate culture stifled American individualism. Men in grey flannel created and expounded the new consumer philosophy of planned obsolescence whilst the Beats turned their backs. 'The only people for me,' said Jack Kerouac 'are the mad ones, the ones who never yawn or say a commonplace thing, but burn burn burn.' The only authentic response to the stifling atmosphere of the times, it sometimes seemed, was to go slightly crazy. But in the teachings of Buddhism some of the Beats began to find a little sanity.[1] Forsaking neat suburban conformity and gleaming consumer machinery in favour of the open road and wild empty spaces, the Buddhist Beats began to forge a new mountain mysticism, a blend of Whitman, Thoreau, Dogen and Milarepa.

Japhy leaping up: 'I've been reading Whitman, know what he says, Cheer up slaves, and horrify foreign despots, he means that's the attitude for the Bard, the Zen Lunacy bard of old desert paths, see the whole thing is a world of rucksack wanderers, Dharma Bums refusing to subscribe to the general demand that they consume production and therefore have to work for the privilege of consuming, all that crap they don't want anyway such as refrigerators, TV sets, cars, certain hair oils and deodorants and general junk you finally always see a week later in the garbage anyway, all of them imprisoned in a system of work, produce, consume, work, produce, consume, I see a vision of a great rucksack revolution thousands or even millions of young Americans wandering around with rucksacks, going up to mountains to pray, making children laugh and old men glad, making young girls happy and old girls happier, all of 'em Zen Lunatics who go about writing poems that happen to appear in their heads for no reason and also by being kind and also by strange unexpected acts keep giving visions of eternal freedom to everybody and to all living creatures...[2]

Prophetic words. The 'rucksack revolution' actually came about not long after, and with it a more widespread existential engagement between Buddhism and Western culture.

Hundreds of thousands of young people in Europe and North America turned on, tuned in and dropped out. Psychedelia; mysticism; Marxism; social and sexual and revolution; protest at the war in Vietnam; the Generation Gap — the 1960s were a time of openness, experimentation, high optimism and freewheeling energy:

... one of those revolutionary moments that seem beyond time and history, a moment that Hunter Thompson described as 'a fantastic universal sense that whatever we were doing was right, that we were winning... And that, I think, was the handle — that sense of inevitable victory over the forces of Old and Evil. Not in any mean or military sense; we didn't need that. Our energy would simply prevail. There was no point in fighting — on our side or theirs. We had all the momentum; we were riding the crest of a high and beautiful wave...' [3]

Buddhism was very much in the air, but it was 'Beat', not 'Square', Buddhism that was right for the times.

Each of you is the Buddha.

said Timothy Leary.

Did you forget that? When they say he's the prince, he's the well brought up boy who went to UCLA. He had a thousand dancing girls or a television set. They kept him from the discovery that there was a way of turning on — of solving the riddle of sickness... age... death. So the Buddha dropped out of school and quit his job and set out on the internal voyage. [4]

The outwardly staid, overtly hierarchical and mainly monastic Buddhism of the East wasn't right for the times. The psychedelic adventurers and social revolutionaries of the sixties were after something apparently more radical. And they got it from teachers like Chogyam Trungpa Rimpoche,

Suzuki Roshi, Sangharakshita, and other figures — some more, some less flamboyant.

The 1960s and early 70s were a time of experimental ferment in Western Buddhism. How were sex, drugs and radical politics going to mix with this ancient, disciplined path? What was the place of women, so long marginalised in the East? How was traditional Eastern hierarchism going to sit with radical notions rooted in Western democratic presuppositions?

Eastern religious attitudes and Western hippie aspirations appeared to constellate principally around one common theme: the idea of liberation, an idea which found its apotheosis in the teachings of Bhagavan Shree Rajneesh, the controversial Indian guru whose identification of liberation with sexual freedom struck a resonant chord with many in those characteristically post-Freudian times. In their attempt to seek out 'authentic', spontaneous modes of being, unfettered by conditioned ego-clinging, the more radical Buddhist teachers experimented with sex, drugs and alcohol.

But times changed. What had seemed to be so innocent in the 1960s and 70s gave rise to reactions and scandals in the 1980s and 90s. The spectre of AIDS, new attitudes to work and wealth, and feminist preoccupations with the imbalances of power apparently *de facto* in sexual relations, created a new, more puritanical, climate.

Much of what was then thought of as radical and experimental is now characterized as 'abusive', and the Western Buddhist world is still in the process of trying to draw appropriate distinctions. Can a teacher never drink alcohol? Is sex between teachers and their students intrinsically unskilful? The debate has been intensified by some of the more shocking manifestations of apparent unskilfulness on the part of some teachers. Trungpa Rimpoche's successor, the American born Osel Tendzin, engaged in unprotected sex with some of his disciples, knowing that he was infected with the HIV virus and infecting at least one of them in turn. The Japanese abbot of a respected Californian Zen centre admitted to being alcoholic. The free-wheeling naiveté of the sixties skidded then crashed.

The revelations of the 1980s rocked many Western Buddhist groups, although the impact of this was felt more strongly in North America than in Europe, and the repercussions are still working themselves out on the Western Buddhist scene. For the radical, experimental ethos of the 1960s and early 70s is only one of the elements behind the crises of the 1980s and 90s. There was also a clash of cultures.

Asian hierarchical authoritarianism, as embodied in some Buddhist gurus and teachers, had operated for centuries within limits strictly circumscribed by tradition. It was clear to those who worked within the traditional frameworks what they could and couldn't do, what was and what wasn't expected of them. Arriving in the West in the 1960s and 70s all these traditional constraints vanished and the teachers were faced with a previously undreamed of plethora of possi-bilities, including the possibility of sex with students who seemed to be so uninhibited, so knowing, free, sophisticated and above all available. Coming from cultures where modesty and sexual restraint (at least in public) were *de rigeur*, it can't always have been easy for them to correctly read the signals being sent by their students.

Western teachers were also subject to unusual pressures. Unused to coping with the kind of authority which many of their students expected them to wield, some of them had their heads turned. Seduced by their own glamour, they started to believe their own publicity. In all of these events, one of the factors which stands out above all is naiveté and where there is naiveté, Robert Bly tells us, the universe will arrange a betrayal. Since this is undoubtedly so we can expect betrayals aplenty on the Western Buddhist scene which, in many places, is still strongly marked by naive romanticism.

One of the contemporary writers who has begun to examine this area is Peter Bishop[5], who explores the encounter between Tibetan Buddhism and the Western Imagination from the perspective of post-Jungian depth psychology and from personal experience of the current Western Tibetan Buddhist scene.

Tibetan Buddhism, he tells us, has touched innumerable surfaces of the Western imagination but, time and again, that imaginative encounter has lead to a literalization of the fantastic—a demythologisation which peels the Tibetan image from its native context and, safely filleted of its complex, messy, shadow aspects, treats the mythic as literal. Despite the apparent diversity of its encounters with Tibetan Buddhism there is a surprising consistency about the way in which Westerners have imagined Tibetan Buddhism and this consistency tells us much about the nature of Western fantasy-making: its dreams of power and its longings for authenticity. Tibet has come to represent the farthest boundaries of the Western psyche, an exemplary standard of all that is enigmatic, imaginatively bold, beneficent and psychically sophisticated.

In all of this Bishop notices a neglected *underside*—both of the Tibetan Buddhist religious system itself and of the fantasies which have reconstructed it in the West.

Tibetan Buddhism is deeply involved in Western problems with the symbolic Father. Time and again Bishop observes Westerners becoming imaginatively paralysed, by-passing paradox and avoiding tensions and contradictions when faced with a benign, omniscient Father image.

He reports conversations typical of the many he has heard at teachings by Tibetan lamas:

Newcomer: He [the lama] didn't really say anything.

Regular: No, it's us that have to listen in another way.

Newcomer: But he just repeated the same thing.

Regular: That's because we have so many blocks he is trying to get through.

Or:

Regular: Did you enjoy the teaching?

Newcomer: Not particularly.

Regular: You came with expectations. When these don't work out as you expect you get angry or disappointed.

Paradoxically, such attitudes are espoused side by side with the injunction not to believe anything one is told but to test it out; to base one's knowledge on experience and not on faith. Western practitioners of Tibetan Buddhism assert over and again that Buddhism is true because it is based on empirical evidence, and indeed this *is* one of the foundations of the teachings. Nevertheless, according to Bishop, this is an *ideal* and not a common-place practice, as, within some communities of Western practitioners, the whole structure proclaims a particular truth prior to any investigation.

The claim to spiritual omniscience, inherent almost by definition, for example, in any reincarnated lama, along with the densely codified iconographic and ritualistic displays of Tibetan Buddhism, create a myth of infallibility and omnipotence.

Tibetan Buddhism, with its hierarchical systems, its elite lineages, its emphasis on spiritual order, authentication and control; its extensive bureaucracies and its determination to ensure its own continuity, all point upwards to the centrality of the Father archetype — the *senex* — personified by the Dalai Lama who sits at the very apex of the system: the last representative of the God-Kings of ancient mythology. In Tibet the Divine Father was always present, *in residence*. He encompassed the whole country, ordered and guided the destiny of the whole nation. But for the West he easily comes to represent the Divine Father whom one *wishes* were one's own.

Many Westerners feel orphaned, without a spiritual Father. The *senex* of their culture either stands discredited (due to ecological disregard, the arms race, global poverty, spiritual bankruptcy), or is absent ('God is dead'; impotent, sick, insane). Small wonder then, that the encounter between these two cultures often takes place in the context of extreme naiveté and over-literalism.

But how to proceed from here? For there is a danger that in trying to get to grips with the problems generated by their own earlier naiveté Western Buddhists might find themselves throwing out the Buddhist baby with the authoritarian bath-water. A new, 'safer' (even sanitised) approach to Buddhist teaching and practice is beginning to emerge.

Ken Jones, a British writer on contemporary Buddhism, contrasts the dangerous 'Charismatic Buddhism' of Chogyam

Trungpa and others with what he describes as an emerging 'Congregational Buddhism':

Congregational Buddhism has had enough of crazy clouds and dragon kings. It is enough that its teachers are sober (in all respects), transparently ethical, reassuringly avuncular ... and account to a board. To all appearances it is a relaxed family affair. It blends the atmosphere of the nicer kind of Christian church with a strong moral tone plus supportive therapy, fellowship and ritual... in brief, the 'consolations of religion'. There may also, however, be the anxious, moralising undertow of political correctness.[6]

and, he goes on:

Enforcing a politically correct sangha is as abusive as the abuses it seeks to remedy. More specifically, Congregational Buddhism is inclined to model the teacher/student relationship on that of the therapist and client, reflecting its more general confusion about spirituality and therapy.

This point needs to be taken further, for it would be a tragedy for Western Buddhism were it to give up the vibrancy and experimental optimism of the 60s and 70s in order to settle down into a cosy *rapprochement* with conventional Western society.

In *Buddhist Saints in India*,[7] Reginald Ray suggests that the 'two-tier' model of Buddhism, which divides the Buddhist world into two chief actors, monastics and lay-people, originally came about in response to a pattern that prevailed in non-Buddhist Indian society. Ancient Indian religious life also had two chief actors: the brahmins, a professional religious clergy, and the householders, to whose religious needs they ministered. As Buddhism started to integrate into the

mainstream of Indian life the original full-time Buddhist practitioners — forest-dwelling renunciants, untamed men and women of the wilderness — began to give way to the more 'respectable' settled monastics and these, seeking ways to influence contemporary Indian religious life and trying to define their place within it, took upon themselves the role of the Brahminical priesthood and began to fashion a 'respect-able', full-time Buddhist clergy ministering to a supportive lay congregation.

Here perhaps we see some of the roots of Congregational Buddhism. As Buddhism begins to integrate itself into the modern West, full-time Buddhist practitioners are casting about for the part they should play in making Buddhism available to others in our society. The charismatic guru figures of the 60s and 70s seem to be discredited. The previously defined Christian roles of priesthood or cenobitical monasticism don't quite fit the bill. In Europe, at least, priests and monks lack social cachet and aren't all that influential — we don't see them on television chat shows very much, they don't write bestselling books. Instead many modern 'professional' Buddhists seem to be turning for their models to disciplines which are altogether more current. Psychotherapists, academic lecturers, technical trainers — these are some of the respected professionals of our times. They are well-paid, have structured, reliable careers, status and influence. How very tempting this must seem to experienced Buddhist practitioners looking to play a part in bringing Buddhism to the West. A new kind of Buddhist hybrid being is emerging from the chrysalis of the 1980s: the professional Western Buddhist Teacher.

These new Buddhist professionals play an important part in a developing, eclectic Buddhist economy. Buddhist centres and

retreat centres need to fill their programmes. They depend upon specialist teachers, who fly in for a day, a weekend or a week, impart their area of speciality and fly out again. The centres' economies depend upon such transient teachers; the teachers depend on the centres; and the students have to look after themselves — for there is no time in the demanding schedule of a freelance Western Buddhist teacher's life for the kind of responsibilities and commitments which the traditional teacher/disciple relationship used to imply.

But there are other factors at work here, for contemporary Western Buddhism is conditioned not only by its own immediate Western Buddhist history. It is also strongly influenced by attitudes which prevail in contemporary Western culture—and we live in interesting times.

The idea of spiritual friendship has always been central to Buddhist theory and practice, but it is a notion which some Western Buddhists have serious difficulties with. For along with the idea of spiritual friendship comes the idea of spiritual hierarchy: the idea that some people are more developed than others and that it is in the interests of those who are less developed to be receptive to those who are more developed. A simple idea, one might think. Not so.

I was once at a Buddhist conference in South East Asia. An American speaker explained how Buddhism is being transformed as it arrives in the United States.

The feminist movement in the United States, she told us, and the strong interest in meditation occurred in the same time period, from the 1960/70s until the present. The contemporary American Sangha, with its understandings of liberation, always joined with the feminist movement and its understandings of liberation.

But now it was time for American Buddhists to go one step further in their quest for liberation and in understanding the feminist contribution. She invited us to think about the logic of domination. The Buddhist tools of mental training, she suggested, are excellent for seeing into the nature of domination and dualism. 'For where there is domination and dualism, there is separation. And this is not true Dharma, because true Dharma is inter-related, non-dualistic, does not separate into higher and lower, superior and inferior, man and nature, us and them. Dharma is inclusive; it brings us all together. Feminism exposes the logic of domination.'

At first glance this might sound fine. Yes, the Dharma is non-dualistic. It teaches the ultimate inter-relationship of things. There is no place for domination in Buddhism — true. But is the separation into higher and lower, superior and inferior, always merely an expression of 'domination'?

What is going on here is that two different levels of truth are being conflated. At the ultimate level, there are no distinctions whatever. No dualism, no domination; no higher, no lower; no superior, no inferior. Also, no speaker, no audience, no conference, no feminism, no Buddhism, no United States — it doesn't make sense to try to speak in this way, as if from the level of ultimate truth, and draw inferences from that position about the way in which we operate at the relative level.

We are not Enlightened. So far as we are concerned higher and lower, good and bad exist. Although the Dharma teaches ultimate non-duality, from the point of view of un-Enlightenment, and therefore from the point of view of spiritual practice, there is a duality between Enlightenment and un-Enlightenment. Unless we accept the fact that we are not Enlightened we can

never progress towards Enlightenment. Only when we have completed the practice and become Buddhas will that duality cease to exist. Thus, whilst we are in the process of practising, there *is* a duality between us and Enlightenment.

Buddhas, of course, don't see things like this. But then they are Buddhas. From their point of view there is no duality between us and them, us and Enlightenment. But we are not Buddhas.

I went up to the speaker after the talk. 'Surely,' I put it to her, 'if we speak of people as being able to develop, then some will necessarily have developed more than others. Granted, we must uncouple the idea of spiritual hierarchy from any idea of worldly power or authority, but not all hierarchies are necessarily hierarchies of power. Can't you imagine a hierarchy of love, or of wisdom, or insight?'

'No,' she replied, 'that word hierarchy always implies power, dominance over others. The whole idea has got to go. It has to be replaced with complete equality.'

We batted this about for a while. Soon there was a group of ten to twenty people around us — all of them Westerners. They looked at me with a kind of benign pity. Here was a rare being indeed: an Anglo-Saxon type of the post-1950s generation yet holding quaintly unreconstructed, antediluvian views. What to do with him?

'But look,' I said 'surely as Buddhists we can all agree that the Buddha and the Bodhisattvas are all more developed than we are...'

'No, I don't like that idea "more developed"', came back the response from someone in the crowd, '*differently developed*, perhaps... yeah, differently developed'.

We fear the idea of hierarchy because we think of it always in association with dominance, and in consequence we bring everything down to the same level. This is a manifestation of absolute value-relativism, where everything has the same value as everything else and any discrimination between values is deemed to be 'judgmental', where that term is used in a highly pejorative sense, implying intolerance and the abuse of power.

But it need not be so. A spiritual hierarchy is just the opposite. The higher up the hierarchy people ascend, the less intolerant they are, the less they incline to any form of exploitation whatever. A spiritual hierarchy is not the same as an ecclesiastical hierarchy. They *may* coincide—that would be a sign of the spiritual vigour of a tradition—but as traditions grow older they tend to ossify and generate self-sustaining ecclesiastical hierarchies. A spiritual hierarchy, on the other hand, depends on nothing more than individual spiritual development.

There are two modes of spiritual hierarchy in Buddhism. There is the clearly vertical hierarchy which exists between the members of the Noble Sangha, who have irreversibly entered upon the transcendental path, and those at lower levels; and there is a more fluid hierarchy, less absolutely vertical, which exists between those at lower levels of spiritual attainment. At this lower level, practice of the path depends upon conditions. Sometimes those conditions are fortuitous, sometimes they are adverse. Sometimes people are up, sometimes they're down. Nonetheless, some of those practising at this level will have had more experience on the path than others. Even if only through having practised for a longer period, they are more easily able to generate and sustain skilful mental states, and they probably have more knowledge of the teachings.

We can always learn from people who are more experienced than we are. Through practising Buddhism, one naturally cultivates a sensitivity to the quality of other people's mental states. One therefore adopts a receptive attitude to those who, whether permanently or temporarily, are further along the path than oneself, and one gives help and guidance to those below. We can do all this quite freely and naturally, in a spirit of kindness and harmony, with neither servility nor dominance. A living spiritual community is in fact a shifting, indeterminate spiritual hierarchy. As conditions change so this shifting hierarchy changes. The important thing is not to be preoccupied with exactly where one stands in the hierarchy — whether higher or lower — but simply to get on with the business of cultivating friendly, sensitive communication with one's companions on the path. Then the question of hierarchy naturally resolves itself as people take what they're offered and give what they can.

That would be the ideal spiritual community. It is not something that all Western Buddhists have a great deal of experience of. There are two chief reasons for this. Firstly, as I have shown, Buddhism arrived in the West upon a particular trajectory, and a very large component of that trajectory was the charismatic Buddhist teacher. Most of the teachers of the 1960s and 70s created Buddhist organisations which centred upon themselves. Their disciples related above all to the teacher and very little to one another. Indeed, if anything their relations with one another often took the form of a kind of sibling rivalry or, in some cases, court intrigue. The relationships of spiritual friendship which existed tended to be almost exclusively those between the teacher and his (in almost all cases 'his') students. Few Buddhist teachers did very much to foster relationships of spiritual friendship at the 'horizontal' level — between the students themselves.

It is as if many of those teachers failed to recognize the parlous state of human relationships in the West today, for we are living at a time of great stress in this area, subject to the strong pull of two opposing social forces: the tendencies to globalization, on the one hand, and increasing atomization on the other. Both of these tendencies are inimical to the creation of healthy, human relationships.

Globalization is characterized by the increasing tendency for the major events of the world to be brought into our sitting rooms on a daily, even hourly basis, devaluing more local concerns and projecting our attention into a world in which we are relatively powerless.

We may know all about the horrors of political violence in Somalia; the famines in Eritrea or the brutality practised against Brazilian street-children. But there is little we can do about them. Yet, whilst some parents sit, absorbed in front of their television screens, their own children may be suffering from an acute lack of affection, or from bullying at school. The dense media saturation that blankets our minds distracts us from immediate and present concerns where we might otherwise be able to act with some effect. To all intents and purposes the media overdose is anaes-thetic: we become inured to suffering — alienated from ourselves and from the realm of what would otherwise be our natural concerns. An overdose of globalization under-mines ordinary, local, human relationships.

On the other hand there is increasing atomization. With every passing year social surveys in the West show that the size of the basic living unit in our society is diminishing. In London today one of the most common forms of living arrangement is the single-person household. In most large cities it isn't uncommon for people not even to know their neighbours' names, let alone have any meaningful contact with them. Moreover, as every day we seem to hear more about appalling, insane acts of violence against children, more and more parents, reluctant to allow their children into the world unprotected, keep them at home: safely plugged into the television network. Allied to this, modern working practices increasingly isolate people at work. On production lines or in offices, many people relate more to their machines than to their fellow workers.

Ever since the last phases of the Industrial Revolution there has been this increasing social tendency to atomization. For most of human history prior to that time people experienced a much broader band of human relationship. There were meaningful, valued relationships between lords and vassals, masters and servants, journeymen and apprentices, teachers and pupils, priests and parishioners, tradesmen and customers. Within their local communities and extended families people had a broad network of relationships to draw upon.

When we speak of 'relationships' these days, however, we often seem to mean only one relationship in particular. When someone talks about 'my relationship', or says that they are looking for 'a new relationship', or that they are having difficulty in 'their relationship', we know just what they mean. They mean their relationship with their sexual partner.

Following from the fragmentation of society attendant on industrialisation, all the complex network of relationships that used to make up a functioning society have broken down. We live in increasingly anonymous isolation from one another and our sexual partners have to bear the brunt of our entire need for human relationships. This puts far too much emphasis on one relationship and too much strain on the other party. Our partner cannot be our father, mother and teacher; boss and buddy; brother and sister; companion and counsellor; guide and sexual partner all at the same time. The sexual relationship cannot take the strain — witness the rising divorce rate.

Social atomisation throws us back on ourselves, producing an increase in self-centredness and self- preoccupation. It has produced the 'Me Generation', with its often neurotic preoccupation with psychotherapy and physical wellbeing; and it has led to a hardening of the self/other dualism, making self-transcendence even more difficult — imprisoned in self-concern, it is not easy to go beyond oneself.

The picture, however, is not entirely bleak. One very positive consequence of social fragmentation is that it gives us a huge range of personal choice. Indeed, it may be easier to free oneself, at least to some extent, from the prison of self-concern than it might have been, several centuries ago, to free oneself from the prison of social structure. This is more particularly true for the women in our society who have a freedom today that their female ancestors only remotely dreamed of.

Because we can now choose to whom we relate—because we are not confined to a pre-determined range of relationships as we might have been in previous ages—we can choose to enter, or create, a sangha: a spiritual community. Indeed, anyone who takes Buddhism seriously, who, however provisionally, Goes for Refuge to the Three Jewels, will need the support of others in their endeavours.

A sangha is made up of men and women who share a common ideal: they all go for refuge to the Three Jewels.

Holding their highest ideals in common they are more easily able to form spiritual friendships with one another.

Broadly speaking, there are two kinds of spiritual friendship. 'Horizontal' spiritual friendship, which pertains to people at more or less the same level of spiritual attainment, and 'vertical' spiritual friendship, which pertains to people at different stages of the path. Ideally one needs both of these. One needs exemplars or mentors — spiritual guides — and one needs friends and companions who share in one's struggles and achievements.

The Buddha himself always went on his wanderings with a close companion. Much of the time he was accompanied by his friend and cousin Ananda. One day Ananda, who had been thinking deeply about things for a while, turned to the Buddha and exclaimed:

Lord, I've been thinking, you know, spiritual friendship is at least half of the spiritual life!

The Buddha replied:

Say not so, Ananda, say not so. Spiritual friendship is the whole of the spiritual life.[8]

Why should this be so?

To begin with, as I have shown, we have to learn the path to Enlightenment in large part from others. This is the way in which the Buddhist tradition has preserved the teachings for the last two and a half thousand years. Teachers have passed on their knowledge and experience to their disciples in an unbroken chain of spiritual friendship which reaches back to the Buddha himself. Without those friendships it would not be possible for the vast majority of us to tread the path to Enlightenment. 'Vertical' spiritual friendships are indispensable.

It is important to remember that 'vertical' spiritual friendships are in fact friendships. This has sometimes been lost sight of in the Buddhist tradition, where Asian/Confucian feudal attitudes deeply influenced Buddhist cultural perspectives. As Buddhism encounters Western cultures, these attitudes aren't present (on one side of the relationship at least). In *The Wheel and the Diamond: the Life of Dhardo Tulku*[9], Dharmachari Suvajra describes something of the relationship that existed between Sangharakshita and one of his Tibetan teachers:

The teacher found that he could also learn from his pupil. Before meeting Sangharakshita, Dhardo Rimpoche had been accustomed to teach in the 'classical' style, seated on a throne while his disciples sat below. Traditionally the lama is regarded, at such times, as the very Buddha himself and it must be difficult to feel anything for him other than profound awe. While teacher–disciple relationships were usually very strong, Rimpoche commented that it was rare for a lama to develop a close friendship with a pupil. Thus it came as a revelation when he realized that something remarkable had developed between himself and Sangharakshita. They had become friends.

'Vertical' spiritual friendships can still be friendships. 'Horizontal' spiritual friendship is also vitally important.

The Buddha once went to visit his disciple Anuruddha, who was living with two friends at the 'Eastern Bamboo Park':

'I hope that you all live in concord, as friendly and undisputing as milk with water, viewing each other with kindly eyes.'

He said to Anuruddha.

'Surely we do so, Lord,' Anuruddha replied.

'It is gain and good fortune for me to be living with such spiritual friends. I maintain acts, words and thoughts of loving-kindness towards them, both in public and in private. I think 'Why should I not set aside what I am minded to do and do only what they are minded to do?' and I act accordingly. We are different in body, but only one in mind, I think.' [10]

Spiritual friendship gives one a context for self-transcendence, an opportunity to put another's needs beyond one's own. It is all very well to insist that our sense of ourselves is ultimately illusory and that therefore we should care no more for ourselves than for others, but it is very much harder to put this into practice. In the case of spiritual friendship, however, one can come to feel so strongly for one's friends that one naturally wants to put their needs above one's own.

Parents sometimes feel this for their children, but parental feelings are rarely simple. Sometimes one feels that one's child is a part of oneself, in an almost literal sense, but the social and biological facts which bring such feelings about have a different quality to them. Perhaps they are more connected with the survival of one's genes, and they often create ties which constrict rather than liberate. Parental feelings are linked up with questions of personal identity in a way in which spiritual friendships are not.

There is also the question of openness. Many people have a private side to their lives which they are unwilling to disclose to others. They may feel, perhaps irrationally, perhaps with good reason, ashamed of certain aspects of their behaviour or, more commonly perhaps, they may simply feel that there are parts of themselves which they cannot express because they hardly understand them themselves.

In the context of deep communication between good friends, however, many of these darker, confused areas can come into the light of day, and one can begin to share oneself more freely. This process of opening up to others is an important part of letting go of a fixed sense of self-hood but it is very difficult, particularly at first, to do it with strangers or with those who don't share one's ideals. Many people experience it as a tremendous relief when they first develop a spiritual friendship and are able to disclose themselves fully to at least one other person.

Finally, there is the question of ethical standards. It is easy to fool oneself in the context of spiritual practice, easy to let things slip and pretend to oneself that some things don't really matter. But spiritual friends help one to keep mutually held ideals alive. When someone falls back, a friend can reach back and give them a hand with encouragement or rebuke. Within a spiritual community shared ideals are kept alive by common practice and commitment even though individual members of that community will undoubtedly slide back from time to time.

Spiritual friendship doesn't come about simply because a number of people follow the same kinds of practice under the guidance of a single tradition or teacher. That helps, but it is not enough. A sangha, in the sense of a flourishing, effective spiritual community, can only come about as a result of its members making real efforts to cultivate spiritual friendships with one another. This is no easy matter and is not something which can simply be left to chance and the workings of Buddhist goodwill. Gone about in that sort of way, one or two people might find themselves sufficiently drawn to one another to begin to forge stronger links between one another, but most will find that their relationships with one another stay at a more or less superficial friendly level. For most people, spiritual friendships need to be consciously cultivated. Like all things, spiritual friendships come about only in dependence upon the right conditions.

For this reason many Western Buddhists choose to live communally, devoting themselves to creating effective spiritual communities founded upon spiritual friendship and, in my own experience as I've travelled about the Western Buddhist world, those communities which seem most successful at generating close, enduring, effective spiritual friendships are those which separate the sexes. Mixed sex communities often seem to degenerate into households of couples and singles, where the singles are often left out of what is most important in the lives of the members of the individual couples.

Time and again in mixed sex situations one sees men subtly competing for the attention of women and women for the approval of men as both sexes project what they most lack within themselves onto those who are most 'other' than themselves — the opposite sex. All of these tensions make for superficiality of contact between people and detract from the possibility of forming deeper spiritual friendships. In single sex communities, on the other hand, people understand one another more easily — they begin by speaking more or less the same language. Even if men aren't quite from Mars or women from Venus, they *are* very different. In single sex situations there is less distance to travel in beginning to create deeper communication (no easy task at the best of times) and, with obvious exceptions, there is less tendency towards sexual distraction and its attendant psychic polarization.

In the end, questions such as these are only going to be resolved in personal experience. Time alone will tell what forms of communal life will be most suitable to the emerging Western Buddhist traditions. But whatever the exact form it takes, one thing is fairly clear. Without a certain proportion of Western Buddhists adopting communal lifestyles with the attendant intensity of friendship and practice that that implies, then Western Buddhism could easily simply become a kind of harmless pastime which some take up at evening classes — like Hatha Yoga, or pottery. For the last two and a half thousand years Buddhism has largely been preserved within practice communities. Western Buddhism discards these more intense foci at its peril.

---

1. Carole Tonkinson, *Buddhism and the Beat Generation*, Tricycle magazine, Fall 1995.

2. Jack Kerouac, *The Dharma Bums*, Viking Penguin, 1972.

3. Jay Stevens, *Storming Heaven: LSD and the American Dream*, Paladin Books, 1989.

4. *LA Times*, Feb 5th, 1967, quoted in Jay Stevens ibid.

5. Peter Bishop, *Dreams of Power: Tibetan Buddhism and the Western Imagination*, The Athlone Press, 1993.

6. Ken Jones, 'Congregational Buddhism and Beyond', in *Roots and Branches: the Journal of the Network of Buddhist Organisations (UK)*,

Number 2, June 1995.

7. ibid.

8. *Samyutta Nikaya*, III.18.

9. Dharmachari Suvajra, *The Wheel and the Diamond: the Life of Dhardo Tulku*, Windhorse Publications, 1991.

10. Abridged from Bhikkhu Nanamoli, *The Life of the Buddha*, Buddhist Publication Society, 1992.

Chapter 8

Buddhist Lifestyles

It is an accident of history that the predominant Western view of Buddhism has, for many years, been based upon a model of the Buddhist life best exemplified by the Theravadin Buddhists of Sri Lanka and South East Asia. Many Theravadins see themselves as belonging not only to the oldest but also to the 'purest' Buddhist tradition and, taking this latter view at face value, several early scholars of Buddhism saw the developments which took place in other parts of the Buddhist world as necessarily degenerative. As Westerners have learned more about Buddhism in general, this opinion has come to be discredited. But the model of Buddhist life which the Theravadin approach exemplifies continues to exert a certain normative influence. For many Westerners (and indeed many Asians), the *real* Buddhist is the saffron-clad monk.

From this perspective, the Buddhist world is divided into two chief actors: monks and laity. The monks are the spiritual 'professionals', following a lifestyle which has been prescribed in great detail by the *Vinaya*, the monastic code. They are celibate; cannot handle money; must not eat after midday; own very little; shave their heads; wear robes of a certain design and carry out certain prescribed rituals on a regular basis. If they do all this correctly then they are seen to be worthy of support by the laity, whose chief spiritual practice, very often, is simply the material support of the monks.

This 'two-tier' model of Buddhist life is characteristically founded upon a belief that the formal monastic ordination as we now know it was established by the Buddha himself; that he personally taught (or approved) the monastic code; and that he himself was a monk in the same sense as those who adopt the current form of monastic ordination[1]. Contemporary Buddhist scholarship[2], however, suggests that the formal *Vinaya*-based monasticism which we see today developed many years after the Buddha's death. Some scholars suggest that its preoccupation with ritual purity arose out of its need to compete with orthodox Brahminism and that its perception of the laity as being of lower status compared to the 'purer' monks may even be a reflection of the Brahminical caste system[3].

The Theravadin model, moreover, is just one amongst many approaches to Buddhist practice. The Japanese Zen and Pure Land traditions, for example, support an extensive married 'priesthood', and had early Western scholars of Buddhism instead first encountered the Tibetan Nyingmapa tradition, with its many esteemed married teachers, the received picture of Buddhism in the West today would perhaps be somewhat broader.

In the earlier part of this century, those few Westerners who called themselves Buddhists, who wished to engage deeply with the teachings and base their lives upon them, had little choice but to adopt one or another of the existing Asian forms. Some went to Japan and trained in Zen monasteries; others ventured to South and Southeast Asia and took ordination as Theravadin monks; or, in Tibet, Nepal and Northern India, they went in search of Vajrayana teachings. From the 1960s, however, this began to change. A critical mass of interest had been reached and there were sufficient Buddhist teachers present in the West for those Westerners who had a genuine desire for the teachings not to have to leave their countries of origin. They could learn all they needed to know right here in the West and many set about doing so with a will.

Over the last thirty years or so the process of 'translation' has proceeded apace. Many different Buddhist groups have come into being, and few of these now follow *exactly* the same forms as those found in the countries of Asia. At the very least most of them have translated elements of the liturgy into the local language and simplified some of their ritual forms. Many have gone considerably further. Most Western Buddhist groups have formal ties to traditions, schools or sects currently found in Asia. Some, like Sokka Gakai International[4], are effectively the Western branches of centralized Eastern organisations. Others, like the Insight Meditation Society in the United States, maintain only tenuous links with their Asian antecedents as they increasingly adapt their approach to Western conditions. In this chapter we will look, very briefly, at some representative examples of such groups: two each from the Theravadin, Zen and Tibetan Buddhist traditions, and I will conclude with a short discussion of the Friends of the Western Buddhist Order, the organisation to which I myself belong and which, unlike the others, does not base itself exclusively on any one Buddhist sect or school but draws on the whole tradition for its inspiration.

The Theravada

In Asia today the Theravadin tradition is experiencing very mixed fortunes. In Thailand the state keeps a watchful eye on the affairs of the monastic sangha and is concerned that, outwardly at least, the monks maintain their 'purity'. Nonetheless, there have recently been a spate of scandals which point to a significant level of religious corruption and degeneration. In Burma, the monks are forced into the invidious position of either (at least passively) colluding with or else, at great risk, actively opposing a brutal, dictatorial regime. In Sri Lanka, several leading monks recently led protests *against* the government's attempts to come to a rapprochement with the Tamil minority[5]; whilst in Cambodia Theravada Buddhism is only now beginning very gradually to revive: the large majority of monks having been killed by the Pol Pot regime.

There *are* points of light in this otherwise bleak picture. Throughout the region a number of Buddhist activists are running effective social action projects for the benefit of the poor and the oppressed. Buddhism is gradually returning to Cambodia; and the Burmese Nobel laureate, Aung San Suu Kyi, is out of house-arrest and is working to put her Buddhist-inspired political principles into action. And the practice of meditation seems to be undergoing something of a revival in Thailand.

The renewed interest in meditation in Thailand was initially sparked off within the Forest Tradition of Thai Theravadin Buddhism, a kind of reform movement, which sought a return to the ideal of spiritual practice (especially the practice of meditation) in wild and lonely places, apart from the large, settled monasteries of the mainstream. The Amaravati Sangha, which was established in the UK in 1976, adheres to that tradition.

Established under the leadership of the American Theravadin bhikkhu Ajahn Sumedho, their training is largely based on the strict practice of the *Vinaya*, whose 227 rules of conduct govern, in minute (and to some eyes, it must be admitted, bizarre) detail, the business of monastic daily life.

Ajahn Sumedho was one of four monks sent by his teacher, at the invitation of the English Sangha Trust, to create the conditions that would support the training of a Theravadin monastic sangha in the West. Since then, this approach to Buddhist training has attracted about seventy Western monastics who, between them, have established monasteries, first in England, then Switzerland, Italy, New Zealand and, most recently, the United States.

There is very little forest left in the West, and one cannot easily replicate the pure 'forest' lifestyle under current conditions. Nonetheless, members of the Amaravati Sangha in Britain have established a number of relatively isolated forest huts which are in constant use and every year many of them go on long *tudongs*, walks about the country, surviving sometimes only on what they receive in alms on the streets of British towns. They also sometimes do traditional almsrounds in the towns close to their monasteries, making do only with what food they receive that day.

Like many renunciants, members of the Amaravati Sangha find themselves caught between two pulls. On the one hand there is the desire to lead a simple, eremitical lifestyle. On the other, there is a pull to respond to the needs of the laity. At the Amaravati monastery itself, this tension is made more acute inasmuch as the monastery has become a focal point within the British Thai, Cambodian and Sri Lankan communities, who naturally see it as a place where they can 'make merit' by supporting the monks and the monastery, and where familiar rites and ceremonies will be performed. A million pound[6] temple project is currently underway at the monastery and this will doubtless exacerbate the tension.

Within the constraints of the *Vinaya*, the Amaravati Sangha have made certain adaptations to their traditional monastic form. They have instituted a form of novitiate as a bridge between monastic and lay life. Candidates for full monastic ordination are ordained first as *anagarikas*[7], and spend time at this level leading a life of celibacy as part of the monastic community whilst not being formally bound by the full monastic code. They have also begun to experiment with new forms for the training of female monastics, which in the highly conservative atmosphere of Theravada Buddhism in Thailand would not have been possible. Relationships between men and women are handled differently in the West. Close proximity between the sexes—even eye contact—is frowned upon in Thailand, but the Western monks allow a little more latitude in this area and their monasteries house both men and women (although the ordained men, however junior, always take ceremonial precedence over the ordained women).

Amongst their Western lay supporters the Amaravati monks don't actively encourage the kind of extreme deference which the Thai laity show to monks, but they nonetheless preserve many of the attitudes of deference, honour and respect which the Theravadin tradition has come to insist upon. Monks eat first at ceremonial meals and always occupy the places of honour, for example.

Whilst the emphasis of their approach centres upon monastic training, the Amaravati Sangha is also concerned with the development of practice for their lay followers — they teach meditation, lead retreats, make an extensive Buddhist library available and give teachings on Dharma practice. They have also recently instituted a programme of 'Upasika Training', which allows lay people to make a more formal commitment to spiritual training.

In adapting their approach to Western conditions, the Amaravati Sangha, more than most Western Buddhist groups, has to resolve a complex set of tensions. They have to reconcile the preconceptions of their local Thai, Cambodian and Sri Lankan lay-devotees (who contribute substantially to their economic support), and the perceptions of the Sangha in Thailand, with the needs of Western practitioners. All Buddhist traditions have their besetting sins and in the case of the Theravada this manifests, perhaps most obviously, as a peculiar rigidity, especially with regard to appearances. The Amaravati Sangha's ability to make adaptations is accordingly circumscribed.

Whereas the Amaravati Sangha adheres very closely to the Theravadin tradition, the Insight Meditation Society, which has its headquarters at Barre, Massachusetts and the Spirit Rock Center in Marin County, California, prefer to think of themselves as inspired by, but independent from, the Theravadin tradition. Between them, IMS and Spirit Rock are the epicentres of a network of teachers and students who practise in what has come to be known as the Vipassana community.

When used in this sense, Vipassana refers to a form of mindfulness meditation that is found in some branches of Theravada Buddhism. The three founders of the American Vipassana movement, Joseph Goldstein, Sharon Salzberg and

Jack Kornfield, studied under Theravadin teachers in Asia. Returning to the United States, they began to teach what they had learned, especially in the context of intensive meditation retreats. They focused very closely on the practice of meditation. As Jack Kornfield put it:

We wanted to offer the powerful practices of insight meditation, as many of our teachers did, as simply as possible without the complications of rituals, of robes, chanting and the whole religious tradition.[8]

Since its first beginnings in 1974, the Vipassana community has indeed brought the practice of meditation to tens of thousands of Westerners. In many respects they have been outstandingly successful. But their approach has not been without its critics. As Ajahn Amaro, a monk of the Amaravati Sangha, now living in the United States, puts it:

Many of the people I meet in America have been doing retreats for 15–20 years and they are really quite accomplished concentrators. But I'm afraid they have not found much freedom.

The reason for this, he goes on to suggest, is an unhealthy separation between ordinary life and retreat.

Of course, if you go on retreats for 20 years you can create tremendous inner space. But it can become almost like a police state. You just clear the streets of all the unruly inhabitants of your mind. And while you may get them off the streets the guerrillas will still be active underground. So when you leave the retreat, you begin to experience your ordinary life as difficult and turbulent. Then you can't wait for the next retreat...

...Even though we might have great brightness of mind or experience of selflessness within that space, those states exist in counterpoint to our family, our society, and the entire phenomenal and physical world. We are losing half the picture...[9]

Moreover, argues Gil Fronsdal, a Vipassana teacher who would like to see the Vipassana Community strengthening its links with Theravadin Buddhism:

It is easily possible that without strong roots in the older tradition the American Vipassana movement will lose its Buddhist identity, melding into our Judaeo-Christian environment.[10]

Zen Buddhism

Although Western knowledge 'about' Buddhism tended at first to centre on the Theravada, Zen Buddhism was the first form to really take hold in the West, coming as it did in the train of Japanese immigrants to the United States. The Order of Buddhist Contemplatives, however, was founded by an Englishwoman.

Based at Throssel Hole Priory in Britain and Mt. Shasta Abbey in California, the OBC, like most Western Buddhist groups, 'aims to remain true to the source of the teaching'. Nonetheless, they *have* made certain adaptations, and with their brown, flowing robes; old-English ordination names (Edmund, Gifford); use of terms like Priory, Abbey, sacristy, vespers and Reverend; their plainsong liturgy and their particular stress on the ontologically positive nature of Buddhahood (which asserts that there *is* an Unborn, an Uncreated) one might think that, outwardly at least, their approach goes too far in the direction of accommodating earlier Christian monastic forms.

Linked through their founder, Rev. Master Jiyu-Kennett, to the Soto Zen school of Japan and the Chinese Rinzai Zen tradition as practised in Malaysia, they have made certain innovations of their own, especially in turning away from some elements within Japanese Soto Zen, where the Soto monastic sangha evolved into a largely married priesthood and where those entering the training monasteries usually do so only for a few years in order to learn the essentials of meditation and ceremonial before getting married and 'inheriting' the family temple (which is then run as a form of livelihood).

Going back to the earlier Chinese tradition, the OBC monks (both men and women are referred to as 'monks' and have the same formal status) follow the traditional monastic code and ordination is thought of as a lifelong commitment.

The lay 'congregation' receives spiritual guidance from the monks and, in turn, provides them with financial support. They are also in the process of developing a lay 'ministry', where committed members give meditation instruction, help to run local OBC groups, and act as exemplars of practice.

Whilst their ceremonial forms are based to some extent on Japanese models, their liturgy (along with plainchant and organ accompaniment) is in English and they have adapted to Western ways in the use of seating arrangements and eating utensils. Along with many other Western Zen groups, they have also abandoned the use of the *kyosaku* — the 'awakening stick' — which is used in Japan to strike the shoulders as a means of releasing the tensions that can build up in meditation.

They have also adopted a more 'open' attitude to practise than that traditionally found within Japanese Soto — their approach tends to be gentler and less formalistic.

Questioning is encouraged, and the need for the individual to retain their own autonomy is given great prominence, but there remains at the heart of the tradition a need for great faith on the part of the disciple, especially when cherished views and opinions are challenged.[11]

The San Francisco Zen Center, which was founded by the Japanese Zen Master Shunryu Suzuki Roshi in the late 1950s, is also based in the Japanese Soto tradition. The Zen Center sangha, a broad community of practitioners which numbers several thousand people, focuses on three practice centres in California — San Francisco Zen Center, Green Gulch Zen Center, and Tassajara Mountain Center. Although they don't maintain formal relations with the Soto hierarchy in Japan, they have recently begun to register their priests with the Japanese Sotoshu and are working with them on translation projects.

The Zen Center approach is based upon the identity between practice and realization.

To practise the Way single-heartedly is, in itself, enlightenment. There is no gap between practice and enlightenment or zazen and daily life.[12]

This approach to the Dharma was popularized in the West by *Zen Mind, Beginner's Mind*, Suzuki Roshi's well-known book. Based on talks given to students and first published in 1971, it remains one of the best-selling books on Zen.

According to Dogen, the medieval Japanese founder of Soto whose teachings Suzuki Roshi espoused, single-hearted practice *is* realization; careful attention to the details of living *is* Enlightenment; in close attention, dualism gives way to non-duality. Dangerous words, for, as Norman Fischer, one of the two current abbots of Zen Center acknowledges, they can lead to a form of bi-polar confusion — justifying, on the one hand, a kind of loose practice in which almost anything can be seen as the Path; and, on the other hand, a rigidly formalistic approach to practice in which the smallest of details are almost comically overemphasized: 'Is the seam of my robe really straight?'. The right approach, he says, '...emphasizes enlightenment without externalizing or conceptualizing it and therefore forgetting that it is in fact present in every moment of our lives.'

Zen Center places great stress on formal practice, emphasizing matters such as deportment, zendo etiquette, and kitchen practice (Dogen is known for his *Advice to the Head Cook*, a tract on the importance of practice in the kitchen). In recent years emphasis has also been placed on communication and working directly with emotions—practices which are not characteristic of Japanese Soto. All of this is done in the Soto spirit, which stresses non-duality (we are all already Buddhas) while at the same time recognizing the clear need for on-going practice. As Suzuki Roshi put it: 'You're perfect just the way you are but it's OK to improve a bit.'

Although their formal meditation and ritual practices adhere closely to the Soto forms (with some chanting in English), Zen

Center has long been involved in the process of trying to clarify the way in which the teaching is conveyed to Westerners. Two key areas are currently under discussion.

The first of these centres on the question of leadership and spiritual hierarchy. Suzuki Roshi's successor at Zen Center, the charismatic American Richard Baker Roshi, was one of the teachers at the centre of a nexus of scandal which emerged on the American Buddhist scene in the 1980s. Accused of sexual misconduct with a female student, and of misusing the power of his position to lead an inappropriately glamorous lifestyle, he was eventually forced to resign from his post as abbot of Zen Center.

The Zen Center sangha has actively worked on finding the lessons to be learned from the various traumas and issues which this affair threw up. What is the place of spiritual hierarchy in Buddhist life? What is the appropriate relationship between students and teachers? In recent years, for example, they have instituted a system of election of abbots by an appointed Elders Council and a democratically elected Board of Directors. Two abbots serve concurrent terms of from four to seven years. Previously, one abbot, appointed by the previous abbot, served for life. The questions raised by this new system (the relationship between temporal and spiritual power, between democracy and hierarchy, between spiritual and worldly authority) are, in fact, questions for all Western Buddhists, for as the overtly hierarchical Buddhist traditions of the East intersect with the currently egalitarian traditions of the West all kinds of cultural clashes have ensued.

The second key issue that they are in the process of addressing is the question of the place of monastic ordination within their tradition. As in the case of the OBC, there are significant differences between the Zen Center approach and that of contemporary Japanese Soto. The Japanese approach to monasticism is more nominal and, having followed that line in the past to some extent, Zen Center now finds itself in an anomalous position where some of its 'monks' or 'priests', despite their ordination, live lives which appear externally to be devoted to worldly objects — home, job and family — whilst there are 'lay' members of their sangha who actually live at the monastery and dedicate themselves full-time to intensive practice.

From the outside, the Soto tradition in Japan appears in many instances to have degenerated to the level of a 'church', occupying itself principally with the formalities of rites of passage. Westerners appear to be approaching the same tradition with generally greater vigour, focusing on practice and the aspiration to Enlightenment. The Soto tradition in America (as represented by Zen Center) appears to be standing at a crossroads where some people look to the Center only to solemnise marriages and conduct funerals while others manifest a strong aspiration to intensive practice and the pursuit of Enlightenment. 'The hope and effort at Zen Center' says Norman Fischer 'is to be able to work with both sets of concerns without losing the power of either: to be able to provide families and individuals with a practice that will deepen their ability to understand and move their spiritual lives, and at the same time to provide training and deep practice for sincere lifelong practitioners.'

Japanese Zen was the major constituent of the first wave of Western existential engagement with Buddhism. It was soon, however, surpassed in popularity by the apparently more exotic forms which came out of Tibet.

Tibetan Buddhism

Its harsh environment and physical isolation, combined with a strong isolationist policy by its leaders and the independent spirit of its people kept Tibet free of direct foreign control for much of its history. A feudal 'theocracy', where vast tracts of land were owned by monasteries or powerful lamas and where feudal serfdom was a fact of life for many of its people, Tibet was nonetheless home to one of the richest and most spiritually dynamic cultures in the whole course of Buddhist history.

In 1950 Chinese forces invaded this mountain fastness and in 1951 a treaty was imposed on the defeated Tibetans which made Tibet a part of China. In 1959, Tibetan resentment of Chinese domination erupted into an uprising which was violently crushed by the Chinese forces and, in 1965, Tibet officially became an autonomous region of China where the Chinese have tried forcibly to assimilate the Tibetans using oppressive policies which continue to the present time.

The Dalai Lama, however, and about 100,000 of his followers escaped to India during the uprising and, shackled in the country of its birth, Tibetan Buddhism now thrives in an international diaspora. The exile community flourishes in India, where some of the old monastic establishments have been re-created (though on a much diminished scale) and there are now Tibetan Buddhist centres all over the Western world.

One of the most vigorous of the Western-based Tibetan Buddhist organisations is the Foundation for the Preservation of the Mahayana Tradition. Founded in 1975 by two Gelugpa[13] teachers, Lama[14] Thubten Yeshe and Lama Thubten Zopa, it grew out of a network of young Western travellers who had participated in some of the courses the lamas had run from their base at Kopan, near Kathmandu in Nepal in the 1960s and 70s. There are now around eighty FPMT centres world-wide with an international headquarters in Soquel, California.

In 1984 Lama Yeshe, whose charismatic style of teaching is widely regarded as having been central to the FPMT's initial success, died and the following year, a Spanish child, Osel Hita Torres, was recognized as his reincarnation. Born to students of Lama Yeshe and ordained as a novice monk at the age of three, Tenzin Osel Rinpoche has now commenced his studies and training as a monk and future master. How this young Western child will finally adapt to his position is a particularly intriguing question, for the re-incarnation of great teachers has long played a central part in the Tibetan Buddhist tradition — how will Westerners adapt to that tradition? How will Tibetans adapt to having Western reincarnate lamas?

The FPMT approach follows the traditional Gelugpa tradition quite closely and much of their liturgy remains in the Tibetan language. They also preserve that tradition's primary division of the sangha into monastics and laity and several of the FPMT residential communities are exclusively monastic.

Like most Western Buddhist organisations, the majority of the FPMT centres are set up around the central activities of study and meditation. Centres offer weekly meditation sessions, weekend courses and retreats of various lengths. They commonly have resident Tibetan lamas and all have qualified students — monks, nuns or lay people — who function as teachers. Many centres, especially those in the countryside, have retreat facilities, and students are encouraged to take regular retreats. More serious students enrol in intensive study programs, in which they examine the works and commentaries of the great masters of the Gelugpa lineage.

The FPMT emphasizes the practice of tantric meditation, to which students are usually introduced in the course of public tantric initiations. There is a growing controversy in the Western Buddhist world about the place of such initiations. The tantric tradition has always in the past been regarded as the more or less esoteric preserve of serious practitioners, and it is embedded in a symbolic context that is quite alien to most Westerners.

Tantric practitioners are urged to see their teacher as a living Buddha and to perform the practice into which they have been initiated on a daily basis, and in some cases more frequently. In the tantric tradition transgressions of these 'obligations' are thought of as leading to rebirth in the deepest hells for many aeons. That is all very well for serious practitioners who have been adequately prepared for such initiations. But today the practices are often given quite freely in the West to newcomers who are not ready to receive them and who are not able to live out the commitments they have undertaken.

Over the years this has led to a certain amount of trauma and confusion, a point that was raised with the Dalai Lama at a gathering of Western Buddhist teachers in 1993. The Dalai Lama spoke out against the practice of indiscriminate public initiation, but undermined his own remarks by claiming exception for his own programme of *Kalachakra* initiation — 'They are very popular. If I just speak on the "Gradual Path" no-one comes!'.

So long as there are students who are taught that such practices are the 'highest' and there are lamas who believe that rather than having the practices die out it is better to scatter the tantric seeds widely, then it seems that students will continue to receive practices for which they are not adequately prepared — personally or culturally.

That having been said, the FPMT is playing an important part in preserving the riches of one of the most developed of all Buddhist traditions and in making its teachings available in the West — especially in the area of study, translation and publication.

The FPMT seeks to 'preserve' the Mahayana tradition. Chogyam Trungpa Rimpoche, the controversial Kagyupa lama who founded the Vajradhatu/Shambhala organizations, tended to take a more radical approach.

Born in 1939 and recognized as the 11th reincarnation of the abbot of the Surmang Monasteries in eastern Tibet, Trungpa Rimpoche's autobiography[15] shows him to have been unusually spiritually precocious. In 1959, shortly after completing his monastic education he led a group of refugees over the mountains to safety in India. Four years later he received a Spaulding scholarship to Oxford University and, in 1968, co-founded *Samye-Ling* in Scotland — the first Tibetan Buddhist centre in Europe.

A brilliant and controversial teacher, Trungpa plunged himself into the counterculture of the late 1960s. In 1969 he gave up his monastic vows and *Samye-Ling* developed a reputation for wild parties, free sex and the use of drugs.

... employing colloquial terms with a poet's gift for metaphor. He was the first Asian Buddhist teacher to plunge into the existential plight of a Western culture and to articulate a way out of that dilemma in the language of those undergoing it.[16]

Amidst growing controversy, Trungpa left *Samye-Ling* and, having married, took up residence in the United States where his 'Crazy Wisdom' antics set a model for Buddhist spiritual life that was 'by turn eminently sane and disturbingly outrageous'[17] His fresh, immediate articulation of Buddhist insights, shot him to fame and notoriety. His book, *Cutting Through Spiritual Materialism*[18], became a bestseller and his organization grew with startling rapidity. He established several rural retreat communities and a network of urban Buddhist centres; created Vajradhatu, a coordinating body to oversee the centres; the Naropa Institute (now an accredited liberal arts college) and the Maitri Institute, a psychotherapeutic care facility. He also gained a reputation for heavy drinking and sexual promiscuity.

Based on visionary experiences of the legendary realm of Shambhala, Trungpa established a 'secular' approach to meditation training, centring on the myth of the 'Shambhala Warrior', which ran parallel to the more clearly Buddhist approach. The symbolism of the mythic kingdom of Shambhala came increasingly to inform all the elements of Trungpa's organization and his own circle began to assume courtly trappings. He became known as the 'Vidhyadhara' ('Knowledge Holder'); his American successor was 'the Vajra Regent'; and his residence became 'the Kalapa Court' — complete with courtiers and a quasi-military khaki-uniformed bodyguard.

Trungpa Rimpoche died in 1987 from alcohol-related illnesses. Three years later, the Vajra Regent died of AIDS amidst scandal and threats of litigation. The events of the late 1980s shattered and traumatised the Vajradhatu/Shambhala sanghas, but they have since begun to recover. The organization is now headed by Trungpa's son, 'the Sakyong' Osel Rangdrol Mukpo and exactly what direction it will move in one cannot yet say.

For all the controversy surrounding Trungpa Rimpoche's life, he seems to have been a remarkably talented teacher, willing to use any means possible to wake his students up. 'Are you awake?' he once asked a student below from the top of a staircase, and, before even receiving an answer, hurled himself into space for the student to catch him. The student missed.

The FWBO

Unlike the other Western Buddhist organizations we have so far examined, the Friends of the Western Buddhist Order does not identify exclusively with any one school or tradition of Buddhism. Founded in 1967 by Sangharakshita — an Englishman who had lived in the East, principally in sub-Himalayan India, since 1944 — the FWBO draws its inspiration from the Buddhist tradition as a whole. Numbering amongst his personal teachers a Theravadin scholar monk, a Ch'an hermit, and several Tibetan lamas (most of whom were known for their non-sectarianism), Sangharakshita is well versed in many aspects of Buddhism.

From small beginnings in the basement of an Oriental antiques shop in London, the FWBO has grown into an international Buddhist movement with activities in more than a hundred locations around the world.

FWBO centres, which are mainly urban, usually have residential spiritual communities associated with them and many are connected with one or another Buddhist 'right livelihood' business. Retreat centres, Buddhist arts centres, complementary health centres, video and publishing ventures have also emerged, as has the Karuna Trust, a fund-raising charity based in Britain that principally funds the work of *Bahujan Hitay* — the social work wing of the FWBO in India.

Rather than initiating all these activities himself, Sangharakshita has preferred to encourage his disciples to develop a sense of practical spiritual responsibility. Most FWBO activities, therefore, have been established, and are conducted, by members of the Western Buddhist Order.

The Western Buddhist Order is a new Sangha — a spiritual community of men and women who have committed themselves to an ever deepening involvement with the Three Jewels. The Order currently comprises about seven hundred men and women around the world. It is neither lay nor monastic. Some Order members choose to be celibate, others not. Some are involved full-time in teaching Buddhism, some work in a 'right livelihood' businesses and there are full-time meditators, artists and writers. Some live in single-sex residential spiritual communities, others hold more conventional jobs and live with their partners and families. What they all have in common, however, is an effective commitment to living in accordance with the values embodied in the Buddha's teaching.

In his approach, Sangharakshita has been concerned not to 'adapt the Dharma to the West' but rather to translate and elucidate. Although deeply respectful of the Buddhist canon, Sangharakshita has always approached it with an open mind, asking 'Why did the Buddha give this teaching? What is its deeper import? How does it apply to someone trying to follow the Dharma in the modern age?'.

In trying to clarify what is most essential in Buddhism, Sangharakshita has sometimes felt called upon to say what it was not, or to point out what he sees as the limitations inherent in certain approaches. This has not always been welcomed. Nor has the FWBO's approach to Buddhism always been well received. For some, the idea of a form of Buddhist ordination that bypasses the division into monastics and laity is simply heretical. Others, concerned with the idea of preserving the purity of lineages of teaching transmission, have objected to the way in which the FWBO draws its practices and inspiration from different Buddhist schools and traditions.

The early years of the FWBO, moreover, coincided with a time of broad social exploration and Sangharakshita approached this period with an open mind and in the spirit of experiment — an attitude which aroused a certain amount of suspicion in the staid Buddhist establishment of the time. But there were so many questions that seemed to be unsettled. Could psychedelic drugs help to bring about genuine spiritual insight? Probably not, he concluded. Was there an alternative to family life? He encouraged the formation of single-sex residential communities. How could one earn a living without losing the intensity of spiritual practice? He encouraged right livelihood businesses to develop. What was the relation between Buddhism and Western culture? He encouraged artistic creation and exploration. And what about sex? The Buddhist tradition has tended to divide the world into those who are celibate and those who are not. But in the age of contraception and with the breakdown of marriage, were there other alternatives? People in the FWBO explored this area to some extent and it is interesting to note that in the past few years there has been an increasing trend towards celibacy, which Sangharakshita has greatly encouraged. A growing number of Order members now choose to follow a more 'monastic' lifestyle.

As with all the Western Buddhist movements, the biggest challenge facing the FWBO today is the question of how it will survive the death of its founder. Sangharakshita has played such a pivotal part in its creation, personally ordaining over three hundred members of the Order, guiding the Order and the FWBO in all its major developments and acting as guide, counsellor and friend to innumerable people along the way.

Most Buddhist teachers in the West have dealt with this issue by appointing a single successor. But true to his emphasis on the importance of spiritual friendship and co-operation, Sangharakshita has begun to hand over his remaining responsibilities to a group of his senior disciples, thirteen men and women who constitute what is known as the Preceptors College. They will provide the future leadership of the Order and the FWBO. The success of this project depends upon the College members being able to work effectively together. For if the FWBO is to survive as a vigorous whole it is crucial that its leaders experience between themselves the same depth of spiritual friendship that they advocate.

Within the next decade or so it is likely that the majority of Western Buddhist groups will be guided by people who have learned their Buddhism in the West. Many of these people are currently in friendly contact with one another and, as I have attended different gatherings of Western Buddhist Teachers, I have noticed a new phenomenon coming into being: Zen teachers practise Tibetan Buddhist meditations,

Theravadin monks study and recite Mahayana Buddhist
sutras, Insight Meditation Society teachers take ordination
as Zen monks. The exclusivity of the traditions which
geographical isolation and linguistic and cultural barriers
formerly fostered is beginning to break down. It seems
inevitable that the Western Buddhism of the future will be
much more of a *melange* than some traditionalists would
prefer. The real challenge facing Western Buddhism today
is not the preservation of the 'purity' of any tradition. What
we really need to be concerned about is that whatever new
forms emerge do so on the basis of genuine spiritual principles and deep spiritual experience.

---

1. See 'On the Validity of Bhikkhu Ordination in Theravada', in *The
Forest Hermitage Newsletter*, April 1994.

2. See Reginald Ray, *Buddhist Saints in India*, Oxford University Press,
1995, and Sangharakshita, *Was the Buddha a Bhikkhu?*, Windhorse
Publications, 1994.

3. Damien Keown, 'History, Holiness, And Hagiography: A New Hypothesis
About Indian Buddhism', in *Critical Review of Books in Religion*, 1995.

4. SGI is a Nichiren Buddhist Organization whose organizational structure is highly centralized. Its headquarters are in Japan.

5. See 'Bhikkhus and Beasts' in *Dharma Life* magazine, Windhorse
Publications, Spring 1996.

6. $1,500,000.

7. *Anagarika* – 'One Without a Home'.

8. Gil Fronsdal, 'The Treasures of Theravada: Recovering the Riches of
Our Tradition', in *Inquiring Mind: A Semi-Annual Journal of the Vipassana
Community*, Fall 1995.

9. 'The Happy Monk: Ajahn Amaro on Living Buddhism in the West', an
interview in *Inquiring Mind: A Semi-Annual Journal of the Vipassana
Community*, Fall 1995.

10. ibid.

11. Rev. Master Daishin Morgan, OBC. Quoted from private correspondence.

12. Yuho Yokoi, *Zen Master Dogen: An Introduction With Selected Writings*, New York/Tokyo, 1976.

13. The Gelugpa is one of the four principal schools of Tibetan Buddhism. Being the school to which the Dalai Lama belongs, it is also politically dominant.

14. *Lama* is a Tibetan word. It is the equivalent of the Sanskrit *guru*.

15. Trungpa Rimpoche, *Born in Tibet*, London, 1966.

16. Stephen Batchelor, *The Awakening of the West*, Aquarian, 1994.

17. ibid.

18. Trungpa Rimpoche, *Cutting Through Spiritual Materialism*, Boulder, Colorado, 1973.

Chapter 9

The Social Dimension

Towards the end of 1994, Pope John Paul II published a new book, *Crossing the Threshold of Faith*. Appearing in simultaneous worldwide publication and in multiple translation, it became an instant bestseller, commercially justifying the $10 million which the publishers were reputed to have paid the Holy See for the rights.

The book raised a storm of protest around the Buddhist world. For despite the Pope's apparent approval of the ecumenical words of Vatican II with regard to the other world religions:

The Church rejects nothing that is true and holy in these religions. The Church has a high regard for their conduct and way of life, for those precepts and doctrines which, although differing in many points from that which the Church believes in and propounds, often reflect a ray of truth which enlightens all men.

in the chapter entitled *Buddha?* he gives voice to, and thereby perpetuates, a persistent Western misunderstanding about Buddhism.

The Buddhist doctrine of salvation constitutes the central point, or rather the only point, of this system. Nevertheless, both the Buddhist tradition and the methods deriving from it have an almost exclusively negative soteriology [doctrine of salvation] [1].

As he understands it (following directly in the footsteps of the 19th century church missionary detractors of Buddhism) the Buddha's Enlightenment 'comes down to the conviction that the world is bad' and the practice of Buddhism involves severing links with the world:

Buddhism is in large measure an 'atheistic' system. We do not free ourselves from evil through the good which comes from God; we liberate ourselves only through detachment from the world, which is bad. The fullness of such detachment is not union with God, but what is called nirvana, a state of perfect indifference with regard to the world.[2]

This classical misrepresentation of Buddhism – that nirvana is a state of indifference to the world – is surprising. It is strange that a man who is in other ways so demonstrably well-read should not know that Buddhist Enlightenment is typically characterized as the fullness of both wisdom and compassion. It is strange that he appears to have no knowledge of the many positive formulations of the Buddhist path and that he chooses to ignore the many examples of Buddhist engagement in the world. So strange is it, indeed, that it is hard not to see here at least the faint shadow of a Vatican anxiety about the growing popularity of Buddhism in Catholic countries.

According to a recent church study, Buddhism is likely to win hundreds of thousands of converts among European Catholics by the year 2000. The countries most 'exposed' will be France and Spain, as well as Italy. Buddhism already has over 100,000 sympathisers in Italy according to the study, which was quoted in the Italian Episcopal Conference Daily *Avvenire:*

Nearly 10,000 Italian Catholics have converted to Buddhism. But Rome fears that one quarter of all Italians share Buddhist beliefs such as reincarnation and others incompatible with the Catholic Faith.

But whatever the Pope's motives, he is not alone in harbouring the remnants of what amounts to a nineteenth century view of Buddhism. Drawn largely from a selective reading of Theravada sources and neglecting much of the Buddhist literature of the rest of Asia, this view was an important strand in the muscular, social-Darwinism which characterized the Victorian view of the world. Here, the 'Oriental mind' was deemed to be passive, irrational, static, world-negating and given to mysticism, whilst the 'European mind' was rational and dynamic —the possessor of superior technology and the superior religion which made that technology possible: Christianity. These ideas justified, to devastating effect, the colonial and missionary policies of the Western nations. Asians, they thought, were largely passive. Their religions taught a kind of quietistic nihilism. It was up to their generous benefactors from the West to bring them the benefits of 'higher' religion and civilization.

This view of Buddhism comes about through mistakenly conflating the Buddhist metaphysical position with its social attitude. It mistakes the voice of wisdom, which negates all claims to absolute existence, for the voice of social nihilism which, seeing all existence as empty and therefore futile, withdraws into solitary quietism. The true Buddhist position is the exact opposite of this. By realising for themselves the truths that Buddhist metaphysics points to — that all things whatever are devoid of inherent existence — ideal Buddhist practitioners orient themselves towards the open dimension. Fearless, no longer attached to praise or personal pleasure, seeing the ultimate interconnectedness of all living beings, they manifest great compassion.

They have set out for the benefit of the world, for the ease of the world, out of pity for the world. They have resolved: 'We will become a shelter for the world, the world's place of rest, the final relief of the world, islands of the world, lights of the world, the guides of the world's means of salvation. [3]

Their internal calm and recollection do not preclude external activities. They exert themselves indefatigably on behalf of all sentient beings whilst at the same time enjoying uninterrupted peace of mind.

Like a fire his mind constantly blazes up into works for others:

At the same time he always remains merged in the calm of meditation and formless attainments. [4]

Given the Pope's views on Buddhism, there is a certain irony in the fact that the term *Engaged Buddhism* was popularized in the West by the Vietnamese Buddhist monk and peace campaigner Thich Nhat Hanh. For Nhat Hanh himself first came to prominence in the West following the campaign which Vietnamese Buddhist monks and nuns launched against the oppressive forces of the Vietnamese Catholic dictator Ngo Dinh Diem. Diem sought to suppress Buddhism in order to make South Vietnam a Catholic state, and some of the most moving images to come out of the 1960s are those of the Vietnamese Buddhist monks who, calmly and fully self-possessed, burned themselves to death in front of the world's press to draw attention to the oppression of Buddhism at the hands of Diem's Catholic regime.

The term *engaged Buddhism*, Nhat Hanh himself freely admits, is something of a tautology. For, given the Buddhist perception of the identity of wisdom and compassion, how could there be a Buddhism which was not somehow engaged with the world? Nonetheless the term has a certain meaning, for there have always been two pulls at work within the Buddhist conception of the spiritual life. There is the urge towards withdrawal, for the sake of meditation, study and reflection; and there are the impulses of compassion, which draw one back into engagement with the world for the sake of all living beings. These twin impulses are contained within the life of most of those who sincerely strive to follow the Buddhist path and the term *engaged Buddhism* can be meaningfully used to describe some of the activities which Buddhists undertake for the sake of others.

Over the last few decades Western Buddhists have established a large number of different projects aimed at taking their practice of Buddhism 'off the cushion and into the world'. One such project is run by the San Francisco Zen Center.

The San Francisco Zen Center was one of the first centres in the West where significant numbers of Westerners began to commit themselves to Buddhist practice. In 1987 it established the Zen Hospice Project in order to bring greater sensitivity and compassion to the task of caring for people facing life-threatening illness. Through its volunteer programs, the project sets out to achieve two aims — to provide residential care for the terminally ill, and a training for carers, aimed at cultivating wisdom and compassion through service.

The directors of the project believe that the giving of care involves one in a two-way process of transformation in which both giver and receiver are changed. How that change is effected, whether for better or worse, depends on the quality of consciousness which is brought to the process. Approached in the right way, care-giving can be a powerfully transformative means of spiritual training.

The heart of the program is simple: bringing together individuals who, through meditation practice, are trying to cultivate awareness and sensitivity — the ability to really listen — with people who really need to be heard. Thus they recruit, train and support care-giver volunteers who provide services at the hospice to individuals during the final weeks of their lives.

It is a mutually beneficial relationship. Volunteers provide practical, emotional and spiritual support — they make soup, change linen, give a backrub, listen to life stories — attempting to bring to these everyday activities the openness, mindfulness and equanimity that are cultivated in meditation. Such responses can transform both the patient's and the care-giver's experience of suffering and impermanence.

The Soto Zen approach inspires another instance of Buddhist social activism, this time on the East Coast of North America. The Greyston Bakery was founded by the Zen Community of New York, initially to support the simple communal lifestyle of its members. The group soon began to take an interest in the occupants of the severely deprived inner-city neighbourhood of Yonkers where the Bakery was located, donating items to local soup kitchens, homeless shelters and churches. As time passed, the Bakery started to train and take on previously unemployed neighbourhood residents and today the Bakery, which now has sales of $4 million, recruits more than 80 per cent its employees from the local neighbourhood.

Through his work with the Bakery, Roshi Glassman, the leader of ZCNY, came to know first hand the experiences of inner-city people. He was especially stirred by the plight of the homeless. It was clear to him that a narrow focus on housing alone could not adequately address the complex socio-economic roots of homelessness and he saw that what was needed was a more holistic approach, which addressed each strand in the web of interrelated causes. Permanent housing was needed to provide stability; jobs and job training were needed to provide reliable livelihood; childcare was needed; as was drug and alcohol abuse counselling; life-skills training; tenant advocacy and a number of other supports which would help to overcome the cumulative problems arising from social marginalization. This vision led to the founding of the Greyston Family Inn, which provides housing as well as a range of ancillary services to forty homeless families.

Two further projects are currently being implemented. A new company has been created to provide employment opportunities for women who have no access to jobs because of a lack of training, experience, child care and transport. And, recognizing the relationship between AIDS and homelessness, Greyston Health Services has acquired a two-acre former Catholic monastery in Yonkers and is converting the site into 35 permanent housing units for men and women with HIV/AIDS as well as an Adult Day Health Centre for non-residents.

All these entities share a common vision — the transformation of individual and social consciousness. Drawing on their Buddhist roots, their approach integrates the spiritual dimension with the economic, cultural and social as they work towards the revitalization of the inner-city community within which they operate.

The legend of Angulimala, which is one of the most popular in the early Buddhist scriptures, inspires the British Buddhist Prison Chaplaincy Organization, which has adopted his name. It tells the story of a young man whose Brahmin teacher demanded a payment from him of one thousand human fingers. Deranged by the conflicting pressures of this demand, the young man became a mass-murderer, waylaying travellers and taking a finger from each. He made the finger-bones thus obtained into a kind of garland which he strung about his neck hence his name — Angulimala, 'Finger Necklace'.

The king ordered a detachment to seize the bandit but Angulimala's mother set out to warn him of what was in store. By now he lacked but one finger to complete his thousand and, seeing his own mother coming, determined to gain it from her. The Buddha, with his supernormal powers, saw what was about to occur and calmly entered the woods to intercept Angulimala. The two of them met and, impressed by the Buddha's steadfast self-possession, Angulimala went for Refuge, entered the Order and eventually attained liberation.

Founded in 1985, Angulimala is recognized by the British Home Office as the official representative of Buddhism in all matters concerning the prison service. Seeking to make available facilities for the teaching and practice of Buddhism in British Prisons, Angulimala recruits and advises a team of Buddhist visiting chaplains to be available as soon as there is a call for their services. It acts in an advisory capacity, and liaises with government chaplaincy officials and with individual prison chaplains, and aims to provide an aftercare and advisory service for prisoners after their release.

As an organization, Angulimala doesn't favour any form of Buddhism over another and has the backing of most major

Buddhist organizations in Britain where it also serves as a
forum for Buddhists of different backgrounds to come together
and cooperate towards a common altruistic end. They organize
quarterly workshops where members report progress, discuss
problems arising from their work in prisons, and study aspects
of Buddhism which are relevant to their common task.

Whilst the Zen Hospice Project, the Greyston Foundation and
Angulimala all seek to ameliorate the difficult circumstances
experienced by some living in the relatively affluent West, the
Karuna Trust in London and its sister charity Bahujan Hitay
('For the Welfare of the Many') in India, seek to help those who
live in the harsh circumstances of Indian social and economic
deprivation. Founded by members of the Western Buddhist
Order[5], these charities are dedicated to the uplift of some of the
least privileged members of Indian society.

Their story is intimately bound up with the life of a remarkable man — Dr. B.R. Ambedkar. Dr. Ambedkar had been born
into an Untouchable family and throughout his early life
experienced the institutionalized prejudice of caste Hindu
society. The touch, sometimes even the sight, of Untouchables was held to be religiously polluting. Living in ghettos
outside the villages, they were expected to perform only the
most menial tasks — removing faeces and the corpses of dead
animals, for example, tasks which were held to be polluting
of caste Hindus. They were only permitted to use certain
paths around the villages, and only at certain times of day (if
their shadows were long they might touch and pollute the
higher caste Hindus). Not permitted to bathe in the public
bathing-tank or draw water from public wells, neither could
they enter Hindu temples; use metal cooking utensils; wear
decent clothes or gold and silver ornaments — all these were
the prerogative of caste Hindus. Nor could they even use the

usual Indian names. Since these often incorporated the name of a god or goddess their use by an Untouchable would bring pollution on the deity concerned and they were therefore forced to adopt derisive nicknames, or the names of animals or birds.

But Ambedkar was a man of great determination and enormous talent. He became the first Untouchable ever to matriculate and went on to gain degrees from London and Columbia Universities. Returning to India, he took up the political struggle against the practice of caste and, despite opposition from such as M.K.Gandhi and other conservative Hindus, rose in time to become the first Law Minister of independent India and chief architect of the country's constitution.

For many years Ambedkar waged an unrelenting struggle to reform Hinduism and abolish the iniquities of the caste system. And although he succeeded, in the constitution, in making the practice of Untouchability illegal, he finally realised that Hinduism wasn't susceptible to the kind of radical reform which he believed was required and that for his people to escape the hell of caste they needed to leave Hinduism altogether and adopt a new religion. For Ambedkar deeply believed in the necessity of religion in society. Despite his strong commitment to the rule of law, he recognized that society was held together more by the sanction of morality than the sanction of law. The function of law is to keep the anti-social minority under control and to prevent it from disrupting the social order. The majority depends for its social life upon the sanction of morality, and this derives from religion.

In seeking a new religion for himself and his people, Ambedkar insisted that it fulfil three requirements: it must be in accord with science; it must recognize the fundamental

tenets of liberty, equality and fraternity; and it must not sanc-
tify and ennoble poverty.

Of all the religions he considered only Buddhism met these
three requirements and, on the 14th of October 1956, tog-ether
with nearly 400,000 of his followers, he took the Three Refuges
and Five Precepts and became a Buddhist. In the days that
followed hundreds and thousands of former Untouchables
followed his example so that by 1957 there were over 4,000,000
new Buddhists in India, a country from which Buddhism had
effectively disappeared in the 13th century. A new Buddhist
revival was underway. What Ambedkar had begun was effectively a Dharma revolution. Carried out by entirely peaceful
means, millions of oppressed people turned to the Dharma as
a means of escaping their former oppression.

Six weeks after his conversion Ambedkar died and his movement was threatened with extinction. But a young English
monk, Sangharakshita, who was living in India at the time
and had become personally acquainted with Ambedkar, was
in a position to take a lead and keep Ambedkar's social and
religious vision alive.

In 1967 Sangharakshita returned to England, where he
founded the Western Buddhist Order and one of his disciples,
the English born Dharmachari Lokamitra, went to live in
India in 1978 where he established the work of the Trailokya
Bauddha Mahasangha Sahayak Gana — the Indian wing of the
Buddhist movement known as the Friends of the Western
Buddhist Order in the West.

Following Dr. Ambedkar's vision that an effective Buddhist
Order would both guide and serve people, TBMSG soon estab-
lished a social work wing in India, whilst in England the
Karuna Trust began to raise funds in the relatively more pros-

perous West (as well, these days, as Taiwan, Japan and Korea). All of this work is strongly motivated by the vision of the Dharma Revolution — the idea that Buddhism can be means for social as well as personal transformation and that entire societies can be changed for the better by its application. To some extent this vision is being realized in the work of TBMSG in India, where hundreds and thousands of previously oppressed people are finding their lives transformed through their encounter with Buddhism.

The charity Bahujan Hitay now runs 19 educational hostels for more than 900 boys and girls in 5 Indian states, as well as 47 kindergartens; adult literacy classes, after-school study classes; vocational training schemes and sports and cultural activities. Education plays a large part in their work because it is one of the chief means by which individuals can raise themselves up in Indian society and, in the context of the extended family, where one person raises themselves up many others – brothers, sisters, parents, nephews and nieces – are helped too.

From its base in a slum district of Pune, Bahujan Hitay runs a primary healthcare clinic and provides facilities for sports, arts, and study to some of the most deprived people in the world. Most of those who use Bahujan Hitay's facilities, like those who run them, are new Buddhists, but the facilities are open to all.

Most of the funding for these projects comes from another group of new Buddhists. Members of the Western Buddhist Order, living in London, have since 1980 raised £5.5 million[6], most of which goes to fund the work in India.

In the context of the Western Buddhist Order / Trailokya Bauddha Mahasangha, both the social work in India and the fund-raising in Britain are seen to be effective spiritual practices in their own right. Perhaps this is easier to see in the case of social work, which requires the direct exercise of compassion, but those who raise funds in Britain also find themselves spiritually stretched in the process. Volunteers join up for regular 'door-to-door fund-raising campaigns', where they will live communally for six or eight weeks, spending their evenings knocking on the doors of complete strangers, explaining to them the details of the work in India and soliciting regular donations. These campaigns require of the volunteers that they maintain a high level of personal self-sufficiency as well as a coopera- tive team spirit. They have to keep their altruistic inten- tions firmly in mind over the period, cultivate clarity of expression and truthful speech, and be prepared to put their ideals on the line in communication with total strangers time and again. Many find that it is the most chal- lenging, stimulating and spiritually fruitful work they have ever done.

So far, we have discussed a number of independent social service projects. The Buddhist Peace Fellowship, founded in 1978 and based in Berkeley, California, is a network of Buddhist social activists who aim to bring a Buddhist perspective to bear on peace, social justice and environ- mental issues.

Beginning as a circle of friends with common concerns and related practices, the network is now much wider and more div- erse, drawing together Buddhist social activists whose spheres of engagement include campaigns against the nuclear weapons programme in the United States; handgun controls; attempts to promote a ban on land mine and weapons production in the United States and Europe; as well as support for Right

Livelihood projects amongst Tibetan exiles in India and Nepal; and the sponsoring of mobile medical teams for the displaced Burmese on both sides of the Thai/Burma border.

They produce a quarterly journal *Turning Wheel*, which aims to express the Network's attitude of grassroots social activism, keeping readers in touch with the wider world of suffering and social activism whilst at the same time reflecting on matters of inner practice.

Their most ambitious project to date is the Buddhist Alliance for Social Engagement — BASE — which is an 'extended practice programme for volunteer social change and social service'. BASE is an attempt to combine the different elements which are felt to be needed for effective Buddhist social action — spiritual community, social action, retreats and training, and spiritual friendship — in such a way as to give the programme's volunteers a deep, effective experience of Buddhist social action.

The programme began in 1995, when the first group of volunteers worked individually in 15–30 hour per week voluntary positions in various social activist programmes in the Bay Area of California as well as coming together regularly for discussion days, weekly meetings and monthly day-long meditations. All of this took place with the support of various Northern Californian practice and retreat centres who helped with the provision of practice space and regularized spiritual friendship for participants. The flexibility of the programme means that it can be recreated anywhere where there are Buddhist resources to hand and projects in need.

The individual projects described above are all to some extent melioristic. They are founded upon the Buddhist notion that actions always have consequences and that therefore both self and the world can always be improved by individual effort. They make no grand claims about the ultimate elimination of suffering, for the problem of human suffering is endemic to human life. All un-Enlightened human beings suffer to some extent, but the ideal Buddhist always seeks to alleviate the suffering of others by whatever means and help them onwards towards Enlightenment.

Having considered the micro dimension of individual projects, we need also to consider the macro scale, for much of the suffering which is experienced in the world today is systemic, resulting directly from the inappropriate management of planetary resources.

Western Buddhists, living in the most affluent societies the world has ever seen, have a special part to play in the unfolding drama of this planet's history, for we are in a position, alongside others, to deliver an urgent message to our society — 'this level of consumption can't go on!'

One cannot consider this area without raising the question of the relationship between economic and spiritual life. One has to begin to talk about money, and this is no bad thing, for one of the important qualities of money, from the point of view of the spiritual life, is that it is a very hard-edged, down to earth, inescapable phenomenon.

The French thinker Simone Weil once suggested that the spiritual life is only really lived at that crucial point which is the interface between the Ideal and the Real. By the Real, here, I take her to mean the mundane, the ordinary, the everyday. It is here that our ideals meet resistance, limit and necessity and it is here that we are forced to take leave of naive, cotton wool fantasy and get down to the real nitty-gritty of spiritual practice.

One can build up all sorts of delightful, soft-focus fantasies about oneself — one's ideals, abilities and insights; one's great compassion, mindfulness and so on — but when these meet the world, when they meet reality and resistance, when they have to be tested in actual practice, then we are confronted by the reality of who we really are.

One meets resistance, limit and necessity in all areas of life, but one where we meet it most starkly is in the arena of economics and personal consumption. The way in which one deals with these issues is vitally important to the way one leads one's spiritual life.

The past decade has seen the collapse of the communist ideal. Almost everywhere, socialism is in retreat and the ideal of democratic, liberal, free market social organization stands triumphant. America and Western Europe took on the Eastern Bloc in an arms race: dollar for rouble, they tried to out-spend one another. Given the relative strength of the capitalist economies, the dollar inevitably triumphed and the Soviet Union gave up, exhausted. The Soviet empire collapsed and 'freedom' broke out all over.

As the succeeding years have shown, however, the first moments of Western euphoria which accompanied the collapse of the Soviet Empire and the re-unification of Germany were premature, for the economic dislocation which these events created in the lives of the newly 'liberated' has been severe. The free market hasn't responded as quickly as its more optimistic proponents expected. Nonetheless, in the absence of any other credible system, we are currently living through a period of free market triumphalism, and this has worrying implications for the state of our planet. For however one arranges to share out the finite cake of world resources, one thing is clear: the world cannot sustain unbridled consumption.

The free market itself is the successful institutionalization of the forces of greed and self-interest. It is simply a mechanism. It knows nothing about justice and cares nothing for conservation. And yet, paralysed in worship at its shrine, our current political leaders seem to lack the will or the ability to regard the crucial issues which press in upon us beyond scope of the market. The most pressing of these issues are global. Over-consumption, over-population, pollution and species extinction.

The world will simply not survive if its future is left solely to the dictates of the market. Yet our society is highly conditioned by the values of free market capitalism; so paradigmatic are they, indeed, that in some circles they are seen as god-ordained. All of us living in the West today are deeply conditioned by its values. We live in highly successful market economies where people are paid far more than they need and consume far more than their fair share of world resources.

Consider the average suburban street in Britain. Each little isolated family unit (these days, on average, husband, wife and one-point-eight children) expects 'by rights' to have access to private housing: three or four bedrooms, two entertainment rooms, at least one and possibly more bathrooms and a kitchen. That is a minimum. They expect to own a private transport system: one or two cars, perhaps a few bicycles. Each little unit will run its own heating and refrigeration plants and they will all contain their own private entertainment centres: hi fi's, television sets, video recorders, video games — a multiplex in every living room. The people living in this street will expect to have regular, easy access to foreign travel (at least an annual holiday in the sun); and they will take the provision of exotic, imported food and drink — bananas, avocados, aubergines, tropical fruit juice and wines — for granted. All this is average and unexceptional. It is also extraordinarily wasteful.

The effect of all this consumption is the increasing destruction of the environment, starvation in places like Africa, due in part to global warming, and the despoliation of poorer, third world countries whose meagre natural resources and labour we buy up cheap on the 'free-market', leaving the exporters, very often, in states of impoverished want. All for the sake of our private, free-market consumption.

The free-market, untempered by higher values, is simply the efficient channelling of the tendency to self-centred individualism, where all people care about is themselves, their consumption, their enjoyment. All this in a world whose natural resources are fast diminishing and where, according to Thich Nhat Hanh, 40,000 children per day die of starvation.

Our political leaders today seem to hold out the vague hope that the free-market is somehow going to sort out the issues of international inequality of wealth and impending ecological collapse. It will not. The free-market as such has no adequate means of inculcating notions of justice, conservation or generosity. Such notions run counter to the very driving forces of the free-market — driving forces which have lent it such powerful impetus and whose harnessing has led it ever onwards to higher and higher levels of 'success'. The market only really understands self-interest, greed and individualism.

In Britain, for example, we have a relatively large, voluntary

sector to our economy. Here we would expect to see the oper-
ation of privatised, market-force-led generosity. After all, we
pride ourselves, as a nation, on our generosity. We individually give more to charity than any other country in Europe.
We give less than one percent of our annual salaries: £7.70
mean average per month, and the big charities are talking
about 'compassion fatigue' setting in.

So far as the really serious issues which face mankind today
are concerned, the free-market economies are like Nero at
the Great Fire of Rome—they consume whilst the world
burns. We have got to do better than that. Urgently. The
changes we have to effect are deep and radical and it is hard
to imagine how our society is going to be able to make these,
but change we will because change we must.

One thing that Buddhists can do is to begin to set an example.
This was always one of the traditional roles of the monastic
community in the East. They set a living example of lives led
happily and effectively at very low levels of personal
consumption. This is something that some Western Buddhists have to offer Western society today — a model of other
ways of living, ways of living which are based in the traditional Buddhist values of communalism. For Buddhism has a
long and valuable history of communal living.

Communalism, as I am using the term, is about sharing and
learning to share. It happens when people get together on a
voluntary basis to share the resources they need to sustain
themselves in a decent manner and where they actively help
each other in the very hard task of changing greed into
generosity. As such it steers a skilful middle course between
the rampant, self-interested, greed-based individualism of the
West and the stagnant, individual-denying, group or state-

based totalitarian socialism of Communism.

The guiding principle of the free-market is 'Give as little as you can, take as much as possible'. The guiding principle of totalitarian socialism is 'Give what you're told to, take what you're given'. And the guiding principle of communalism is 'Give what you can, take what you need'.

It has been natural for many of the Western Buddhist groups, which took root in the 1960s, at a time of social experimentation and the communal idealism, to carry those experiments over into their Buddhist lives. Thirty years on, they have a learned a great deal and have much to offer in the way of practical experience. It is worth looking at an example of one such communal situation in greater detail.

Windhorse Trading, which is based in Cambridge, England, is a Right Livelihood enterprise which was founded in 1981 by members of the Western Buddhist Order. They import handicrafts, mainly from Asia, and (having checked that the goods are produced in a non-exploitative manner) retail and wholesale them across Britain and in other parts of Europe. From small beginnings on a market stall in London, Windhorse Trading has grown into an enterprise which, at the time of writing, has annual sales of £5.5 million[7] and employs 150 people.

All of the people who work in the company are Buddhists, who see their work as a means of putting Buddhist ideals into practice in the world. For the work itself — when combined with a daily meditation practice, Buddhist study, six weeks of annual retreat and community living — is an effective spiritual practice in its own right. Training in work as a spiritual practice, the members of Windhorse Trading learn to apply Buddhist ethics in practice and to bring a high level of mindfulness to their tasks. They learn to co-operate and communicate with others; to put forth energy to overcome obstacles; and to cultivate generosity — for their system of remuneration is based on the ideal of 'give what you can, take what you need'. An unmarried executive director of the company, living in one of their communal households, takes home the same 'pay' as most other workers whilst someone working on the warehouse floor, who has a family to support, takes considerably more. Taking little for themselves, living simply, the workers at Windhorse Trading make surplus profits available to fund Buddhist activities around the world.

A financier with whom they do business recently described the lifestyle of those working at Windhorse trading as one of 'designer poverty' — an apt expression.

To illustrate the idea of designer poverty, take the example of a single person, working for the business and living in one of their communities. In cash or kind, he or she receives about £6,000[8] per annum. This is less that half the average income in the UK. It hovers close to what some social statisticians would classify as a 'poverty line'. By the standards of the wider society they are definitely poor. But how does it look to them?

For this £6,000 they get a room in a comfortable, pleasantly furnished, centrally heated house; £25 per week spending money; easy access to communications facilities; use of a shared car; a minimum of six weeks of paid retreat per year; good, regular meals; and, perhaps above all, they get the sense that they are able to give what is surplus to their needs to causes which they believe in. If they genuinely need more, they can ask for it and be sure of receiving a sympathetic hearing from their fellow-workers.

Communalism is an economically efficient way of living. Thirteen people share one mortgage; one washing machine, spin-dryer, telephone, cooker and fridge. Fifty people share six cars. And so on. Major ecological consequences flow from this. People working in Windhorse Trading, living communally, take fewer of the world's scarce resources, destroy less of the world's ecology, and are by and large materially content.

The wider society might judge them poor but they are really quite well-off. Although they are 'poor' their lives are comfortable, creative and generally fulfilled, for generally speaking, their sense of identity, of self-worth, tends to derive more from what they can do for others than it does from what they have for themselves. This is both healthy and unusual, for in our society today money plays an unduly large part in most individuals' sense of self-worth. For we are bewitched by money.

Money is a peculiar phenomenon. However hard one looks for it, one can never find the thing itself: all that appears are tokens — bank notes, coins, promissory notes, cheques, or electronic data on a computer. Few of these have any intrinsic worth and yet they can all be turned into things far more valuable than they are in themselves. Money *is* only as money *does*. It takes shape when purchases occur, when individuals express choices and exchange tokens for apparent benefits. But those tokens are so alluring. Being almost infinitely elastic (money can seem to buy almost anything) they have immense potency: for money is pure potential.

This apparent potency appeals immediately to each individual's sense of lack. We are incomplete. Our identity is never fixed and final. In the face of chaos and change, the ever-transient flux of conditions, we try to take hold of whatever will provide us with a secure sense of identity. But nothing is ever secure, things keep on changing, and we experience a continuous sense of lack. There is always something missing. But money seems to be able to become anything. If we have enough money then surely we will be able to fulfil our sense of lack? Money can become anything: motor cars, food, beautiful interiors, culture, sex. It can buy all this and more: surely it can provide real security? If money can't, nothing can. Too true, nothing can. Our sense of lack can never be fulfilled at its own level.

On the physical plane, one's desire for material security can never be achieved. The fact of universal impermanence makes that impossible: everything always breaks down. On the psychological plane, one's quest for a secure sense of ego-identity can never be fulfilled. Like a house built on sand, the foundations shift and the structure falls every time one builds it up. Bewildered by the workings of universal impermanence and the inherent fragility of ego-identity, we become bewitched by money and money ends up enslaving us.

Despite the unprecedented material abundance most people in our society experience they are still willing to give up what they want and what they really enjoy — time, leisure, contact with friends and family, the feel of the breeze and the sound of bird-song — to shut themselves off, doing soul-destroying jobs in arid environments; slaving away to acquire vast numbers of empty tokens which promise everything. Most people in our society have far more than they ever need but the system of money-slavery which we have set up seems inescapable. We can always get more, and that is so very alluring.

There is only one solution to this. To give it up. The simple way out of money-slavery is to become voluntarily poor.

Recognizing that once one has met the basic requirements for a healthy human life: adequate food, clothing, shelter and culture for oneself (and one's dependants) one needs no more on the material plane, and one can then lead a life of voluntary 'poverty'. Taking no more than one needs one is free to give what one can, willingly sharing resources with others for the sake of all.

Designer poverty is poverty 'by design'. People can enter into it willingly once all their real material needs are met. But there is another element to it. It is *designer* poverty. There is an aesthetic element implied here. This aesthetic element is very important. You don't need to be rich to dress with style and taste. Nor do you need to be rich to take care of your physical environment and put thought and care into it. All you need are few quite limited material resources, a bit of aesthetic sensibility, a bit of imagination and some self-esteem.

I myself have lived such a lifestyle for the last twenty or so years and never in all that time have I ever thought of myself as in any way impoverished. The reason for this is that the things which really matter to me, the things which really enrich me, are either free or else, like books and music, they are reasonably cheap and accessible.

Friendship, meditation, human communication, walks in the country, art galleries and museums (in Britain at least) are free or reasonably cheap. The appreciation of litera-ture, music, art and architecture is free. One does not need enormous sums of money to have access to art and culture. Those things that truly enrich us, that make human life worth living, do not require vast surpluses. Despite having been supported at a relatively low economic level I have always had easy access to them. I have had far easier access to them, in fact, than I would have had I been trying to hold down an ordinary job.

Everything is interconnected. This Buddhist metaphysical position can be seen very clearly in the context of our ordinary economic lives. Turning on a light-switch, we take part in a process which causes sulphuric fumes to rise from the electricity generating power station which supplies us with our sixty watts and we play a direct part in the creation of acid-rain. Starting the engine of a car we send greenhouse gasses into the upper atmosphere and play a direct part in the deadly process of global warming. Buying an ordinary white tee-shirt, we play a part in the pollution of a river somewhere with bleach and help to perpetuate a system of sweat-shop labour in the factory which made the shirt. And so it goes — on and on. So long as we live in the modern West we are, from second to second almost, party to environmental destruction and economic exploitation.

The economic world today is vast beyond comprehension. It is an ocean of money, almost without limit. It is hard to see how, in the face of a world of this magnitude, small enterprises like Windhorse Trading can make very much difference. It is all too easy to sink into a slough of pessimism. But one must not be too impatient. Positive changes come about through individuals and institutions modelling themselves on positive examples. It takes time for the lessons these provide to be seen and to be acted upon. In the meantime, however, those who are working at creating saner ways of life, for themselves and others, derive immense personal benefit from the process. An enterprise like Windhorse Trading may not change the world overnight, but it has much to offer those who would look and, in the meantime, enterprises like these provide invaluable conditions for practice to hundreds of people.

There is a tendency on the part of some Western Buddhists to believe that the world is best left to look after itself. Buddhists should simply get on with their spiritual practice. Those who genuinely seek the teachings will come of their own accord. This view is close to a state of callous indifference to the sufferings experienced by so many. Western Buddhists have an enormous amount to offer the world today. Above all, perhaps, they can offer a vision of a path to happiness which is not posited on the endless accumulation of material benefits.

We live in a society, most of whose members enjoy wealth, power and luxury beyond the dreams of medieval princes (air travel, motor cars, credit cards, central heating and air-conditioning) whilst being simultaneously oppressed by a constant sense of present scarcity: one can never get enough. In all of this, perhaps the most effective means of social engagement that Western Buddhists can undertake is to get out into society and make the Buddha's teachings available — open-handedly offering others the means to achieve a saner way of life; for the sake of themselves, for the sake of all.

---

1. Pope John Paul II, *Crossing the Threshold of Hope*, Alfred A. Knopf, 1994.

2. ibid.

3. *Astasahasrika 15:293* from *Buddhism: its Essence and Development*, Edward Conze, 1959.

4. *Ratnagotravibhaga, 1.73.*

5. In India the Western Buddhist Order is known as the Trailokya Bauddha Mahasangha.

6. $8.25 million.

7. $8.25 million.

8. $9,000.

Chapter 10

Buddhism and Western Culture

The Convent of Santa Croce stands on a hill near the village of Batignano in the rolling Tuscan countryside. Juniper and holly-oak dot the hillsides, goats graze under ancient, twisted olive trees and the summer skies are pure cobalt blue. It is many years since the convent was used by Christian monastics, but for much of the 1980s its quiet, cloistered atmosphere made it an ideal venue for the three month ordination retreat run every year by members of the Western Buddhist Order.

Ordination retreats are a time of intensive training. Silence, meditation and ritual are interspersed with periods of study and reflection. For those attending, these retreats are the culmination of long-cherished aspirations. Some of them may have been training for ordination for as long as ten years and now, in a ceremony imbued with deep symbolism, they will finally enter the Order.

Those Tuscany retreats were like a tiger's cave. You went in and never came out again. The people who left the retreat after three months were never the same as those who had begun it. There was a kind of glow to them, as if the Tuscan summer had caught them up and made them its own. They all came back with tales of high points, moments of heightened significance which, you could see, would remain deep within them and inform their lives for many years to come. And for some, strange to say, the highest of these high points occurred after the ordinations and after the retreat when, with their senses cleared and purified, they made their way to Florence and encountered, in all their grace and glory, the spiritual treasures of the Italian Renaissance.

As it made its way through Asia, Buddhism usually brought culture with it. In Tibet, according to legend, it even brought the art of writing. Only in China did it come upon a civilization similar in the extent of its prior cultural development to our own. There Buddhism played a major part in the cultural renaissance which marked the T'ang dynasty, producing one of the most magnificent civilizations the world has ever seen. Rather than turning us away from what is best in Western culture, Buddhism can help to return us to it, for the West today is in the grip of a major cultural crisis of confidence.

In this chapter I will look at different aspects of the relationship between Buddhism and Western culture, particularly in the fields of art, science, philosophy, psychotherapy and religion, for in each of these fields Buddhism brings something distinctive to bear and offers the prospect of a radical re-visioning.

Ever since the start of the nineteenth century, with the birth of Romanticism, Westerners have sought a spiritual and cultural renaissance from the East. 'In the Orient' said Friedrich Schlegel, one of the founders of the Romantic movement 'we must seek the highest Romanticism'.

Oriental Romanticism scattered seeds of influence in all directions. Schlegel influenced Schopenhauer (who kept a figure of the Buddha, along with a bust of Immanuel Kant, on his desk) and Schopenhauer influenced Nietzsche and Wagner (Wagner started on an opera based on the life of the Buddha). In America, the New England 'Transcendentalists' vigorously took to the new Orientalism (E. P. Peabody rendered a French translation of *The Lotus Sutra* into English) and in England, Sir Edwin Arnold's poetic rendition of the life of the Buddha, *The Light of Asia*, sold in hundreds of thousands.

'Whoever knows others as well as himself,' wrote Goethe in the early 19th century 'must also recognize that East and West are now inseparable'.

The conjunction of orientalism and Romanticism was nothing new. Europe's loss of faith in her rational traditions in the 2nd century had also ushered in 'a vogue of oriental prophets' with the rise of gnosticism. But the Romanticism of the early 19th century marked the beginnings of a self-doubt that could not be dismissed as an aberration and each time Europe was seized with another attack of it (in the 1870s, 1920s and 1960s), it was always accompanied by a further wave of enthusiasm for the East. [1]

'O Grand Lama' wrote the despairing dramatist Antonin Artaud to the Dalai Lama in 1925, 'give us, grace us with your illuminations in a language our contaminated European minds can understand, and, if need be, transform our Mind...'

Cultural self-doubt has now become virtually a way of life. The old moral and aesthetic certainties have given way to mere opinion and the idea that there could be a hierarchy of values has been overtaken by the widely held conviction that all values are only relative, that nothing is really worth much more than anything else, that it all just depends on your point of view.

This state of complete value-relativism is culturally and spiritually enervating. At the same time, it looks superficially similar to the Buddhist position, for Buddhism also asserts that values are relative, that our feelings, thoughts and beliefs all arise in dependence on conditions. If everything is just conditioned, how can you say some things are better than others? It all just depends on your conditioning.

'You like Shakespeare, I like soap-operas. So what?'

Buddhism, however, is more subtle than that and its response to this problem points to a way out of the morass in which much of our culture is currently mired.

Everything *is* conditioned, but conditionality, as we saw in chapter 3, can operate in two different modes. There is cyclic conditionality, where one mental state gives way to another on a plane of more or less horizontal value; and there is spiral conditionality, where, in dependence upon one positive mental state, another, even more positive, is produced.

Convinced, consciously or otherwise, that we have a fixed, separate self-hood, the propensities which have gone into making us what we are now present the world to us in a particular way. Responding to that presentation with craving or aversion, we cling to the pleasant, thrust away the unpleasant, and thus perpetuate the process of 'being who we are', confined within a mono-dimensional band of more or less familiar experience.

Intuiting the ultimately unsatisfactory nature of this process, we can instead try not to give way to craving and aversion. Maintaining a clear awareness of our feelings and sensations, we can open out the gap between feeling and craving. This experience strengthens our intuition of how things really are and a series of ever more intensely positive mental states therefore follow. In that moment between becoming aware of a feeling and giving way to craving, the open dimension, which is always present, is made more explicitly manifest and we can turn towards it, or away from it.

Greed and self-preoccupation preserve a delusive belief in the reality of our ultimate separation from others. Generosity and concern for others correspond more closely to the reality of interconnectedness. From these facts of life we can deduce a hierarchy of values which is ordered in accordance with how things really are. The more things accord with reality, the higher in the hierarchy they stand. Generosity stands higher than greed.

There is an ethical dimension to this hierarchy (generosity is better than greed) and there is an aesthetic dimension, for just as one can respond to the world by taking or by giving, so one can respond to it in a spirit of appropriation or appreciation.

My teacher tells a story from his time in India to illustrate this. He was walking with an acquaintance in the Himalayan town of Kalimpong, when his attention was struck by a majestic tree growing by the roadside.

'Just look at this magnificent tree...' he said to his companion.

'Oh, yes! It would make so *many* bundles of firewood!' his companion replied.

We can see things with the eye of aesthetic appreciation, where we see things 'in themselves', as they are, without relation to us and our needs; or we can see them only as they relate to our needs and desires. To experience something as beautiful is to be lifted for a time out of our normal rut of self-concern into a quite different world — one which is concerned with values rather than interests.

The very idea of beauty, however, especially in relation to works of art, is under attack in our culture today, where all values are sometimes thought to be entirely relative, depending on nothing more than the interwoven fabric of economic, social and historical conditions. At one extreme, this point of view would suggest that the 1997 Stratford-upon-Avon telephone directory has no less an intrinsic value than the complete works of that town's most famous son, William Shakespeare. Both of these 'texts' are just collections of black marks on white paper and the interpretations we give to them are determined entirely by the accidents of history which itself is simply the saga of the conflict between different social, political and economic interest groups.

Absurd as such views may seem, opinions not unlike this have strongly taken hold in our modern academies, where, as the American literary critic Harold Bloom puts it:

I feel quite alone these days in defending the autonomy of the aesthetic, but its best defence is the experience of reading King Lear and then seeing the play well performed. King Lear does not derive from a crisis in philosophy, nor can its power be explained away as a mystification somehow promoted by bourgeois institutions. It is a mark of the degeneracy of literary study that one is considered eccentric for holding that the literary is not dependent upon the philosophical, and that the aesthetic is irreducible to ideology or to metaphysics... [2]

This is a great loss, for the experience of great music, art, literature and drama can be spiritually transforming. The experience of beauty — that state of expansive egolessness, where one is drawn beyond one's petty concerns and preoccupations, into a quite different world, alive with colour and significance — is a vital part of spiritual practice.

Transcendental reality is ineffable. It is beyond the horizon which delineates our current state of consciousness. But the urge to get to grips with that reality is latent within all of us. For much of our history, that urge expressed itself in the creative struggle of artists to form imaginative representations of their own most intense experiences. The images they created populated the Western imagination, creating a vivid world of heightened significance, intermediate between transcendental reality and every day life. The world of poetry, myth and legend expresses this sense of heightened significance. Engaging with it, we are lifted out of the rut of our petty concerns and, for a time, our lives are imbued with greater depth and meaning. The images which are brought forth in this dimension often embody deep, unconscious elements within the psyche and by engaging with them we can move towards a higher level of psychic integration.

The imagination, however, is not to be identified solely with the archetypal, mythological world which tradition brought forth. Engagement with the vivid world of mythological archetypes is spiritually and psychologically rewarding, but the world of the imagination is not confined to this realm alone. Rather, it is universal, for our world is made up of nothing but images.

To see anything as it really is is to see it as an image. There are no 'things', all we have are momentary representations, fleeting significations generated within the great flux of conditions. Everything our senses present to us is a signification, an image of reality. But we tend to treat the world (and ourselves) as finite and enduring. We see 'things', not images. We don't see chairs, tables, ants, specks of dust or flowers, imbued with their true significance. They don't see them as signifying reality.

Once, instead of giving a discourse, the Buddha held up a golden flower, smiled and said nothing. His disciple, Maha Kashyapa, smiled back and the Buddha saw that Kashyapa knew.

The arts at their best present images *as images*.

One of my favourite pictures is Vermeer's 'Milkmaid'. She stands over a basin, pouring milk from a jug. An ordinary serving woman doing a simple daily task. But the picture is marked by a quality of translucent, transcendent, tranquillity. The ordinary world, we see, is marked with the pure radiance of reality, it is not a world of leaden, separate 'things'. This picture is the product of deep sympathy and profound aesthetic appreciation, it is a gateway into that dimension where the light of reality shines in every appearance. Contemplating it, I find I can, for a time, lose myself altogether.

To the extent that one engages with the imaginative dimension, to that extent one slips the bonds of subject–object duality.

Today, however, the arts are bewildered. Seduced by the siren calls of pseudo-egalitarianism ('Who has the *right* to make aesthetic judgements?') they have foregone the vital sense of aesthetic appreciation. It is part of the current malaise that the word 'beauty' leaves many of today's art students simply confused. Turning their back on the riches of the Western imagination, many of today's artists confine themselves to producing clever, ironic, 'comments' on the state of the world or themselves. There is no struggle here, little imagination and no beauty. It has all gone somewhat flaccid.

The two Buddhist ideas that I've outlined, that there is a natural hierarchy of values and that reality is perceived in the imagination, contain within them the seeds of a Western cultural renaissance. They return us to a sense of the value of aesthetic experience and point us back to the imaginative riches of our Western cultural heritage.

But Buddhism does not encounter Western culture in the realm of the arts alone. It also addresses the world of science.

For the last three hundred years in the West, the worlds of art, science and religion have come to speak languages founded upon entirely different grammars. The world of scientific method speaks a different language to that of belief-based monotheistic faith which is different again from the secular language of human-centred art. As a result, these three areas have increasingly drifted apart and this process has added to the fragmentation and dislocation of the Western imagination. In Buddhism, however, art and science can proceed upon the same grammar, for there is nothing in the language of conditionality which offers resistance to either.

Buddhism entered Western cultural life along with eighteenth century romanticism. But there is nothing intrinsically 'romantic' about Buddhism and it is interesting to speculate what might have happened had Buddhism first been encountered by 17th century Rationalists rather than 18th century Romantics. Focusing on entirely different elements within the Buddhist tradition — the *Abhidharma*, perhaps, with its highly detailed working out and classification of the components of existence — the 17th century would have produced a very different style of Western Buddhism.

The Buddhist approach to spiritual life is thoroughly experiential. The Buddha himself regarded no data, however mundane, as irrelevant to his teaching of conditionality and he drew, for teaching purposes, on whatever his era knew of natural phenomena. In contrast to other teachers of the time, he regarded himself as an empiricist, relying only on that which is known and testable in experience. The interdependence that he saw between the mental and the physical and between thought and perception broadens those areas of enquiry to which his teachings can be seen to be relevant.[3]

Buddhism has arrived in the West at a time when the one-way causal paradigm of classical science (A causes B causes C) is beginning to be seen as increasingly inadequate in resolving scientific problems and making sense of scientific evidence. The principle of conditionality replaces the idea of linear causality with the notion that events arise, never in dependence on any single cause, but rather as a consequence of an infinite conflux of interacting conditions.

This idea has strong resonances for a new branch of scientific thought called Systems Theory. Systems theorists replace the idea of one-way causality with the idea that all wholes — animals, vegetables, cells, organs or organisms — are best described as systems. Systems are not so much 'things' as patterns. Their character derives less from the nature of its components than from their organisation[4]. As such, it consists of a dynamic flow of interactions, rather as I demonstrated with the image of my *Lavatera* 'Barnsley'. There are no 'things', there are just temporary patterns.

This idea can be applied to such diverse spheres as physics, biology, psychology, cognitive science, ethics, economics, politics and sociology. Perhaps most importantly, it is central to the rapidly developing science of ecology, where its import in terms of describing our relationship to our world has been expressed most clearly in the 'deep ecology' movement.

Deep ecologists eschew the short-term, technology based approach to ecological problems which focus on cleaning up, say the Hudson River or the Thames for the sake of our own species alone. Setting ourselves up apart from the world in this way, they say, does not address the fundamental nature of the problem, which is the nature of our relationship to the world. What is destroying the world is our persistent belief that we are independent of it, aloof from other species and immune from what we do to them.[5]

Theories founded upon linear causality have proved to be very effective ways of thinking about certain highly specific issues. But it is an approach which also makes for highly artificial divisions within reality by focusing exclusively on a limited set of attributes of the matter under investigation.

Economists, dealing only with certain limited factors within an overall situation, have come at times to speak of people as 'units of production'. Their intrinsic humanity, their complex of relationships, joys and sorrows is of little consequence when considering the economic models that are predicated exclusively upon linear causality: these are not, and cannot be, thought of as relevant data within an exclusively linear system of thought. We have therefore produced a 'human science' which can at times be numbing in its inhumanity.

Our fixation upon linear causality has created a world where physicists are not expected to account for the ethical implications of their work or bankers for the environmental implications of their loans.

Linear causality has played an enormous part in the creation of the modern world. It has helped to deliver vaccines as well as atomic bombs; cures for cancer as well as the greenhouse effect. The Buddhist view of universal interconnectedness, brought to bear upon modern scientific method, would shape the world very differently. It would not only provide more satisfying answers to some scientific conundrums. It would also help us to see that the consequences of actions and events are never simply linear, they resound in all directions. And it is vitally important that the scientists whose work influences every dimension of our daily lives come more deeply to acknowledge the reality of this interconnectedness — a reality whose import passes crucially from the theoretical into the ethical and practical domains of modern life.

The abstraction from the processes of daily life which marks the world of modern scientific research also characterizes the world of contemporary philosophy, and although some philosophers have turned their attention to Buddhist thought over the last two centuries, their approach has generally been flawed by the persistence of their own presuppositions.

The encounter between Buddhism and Western philosophy, not surprisingly, usually centres on one or another of the great 'thinkers' of the Buddhist tradition. The figure most often selected is Nagarjuna, the second century Buddhist scholar-saint whose teachings form the basis of the Madhyamaka School of Mahayana Buddhism. But the way in which Western philosophers have read Nagarjuna says, perhaps inevitably, more about them than it does about Buddhism.

The story begins with Schopenhauer and other nineteenth century idealist philosophers who saw Indian thought as a response to the problem of the relation of appearance to reality and therefore read Nagarjuna as if he were a Platonic or, more usually, Kantian transcendentalist. In the early twentieth century, Western logical positivist philosophers were more concerned with questions of causal efficacy and logical accuracy. They saw Nagarjuna as a logical analyst. Subsequently, after Wittgenstein, he has been seen as an antiphilosopher, primarily concerned with the use of language, conceptual holism and the limits of philosophical discourse[6]. More recently, the emphasis has been on the relationship between Buddhism and postmodern thought, and Nagarjuna is seen to have resonances with the thinking of Jacques Derrida.

But none of these approaches have taken into account the fact that Nagarjuna was not just a thinker. He was primarily a religious *practitioner*. We know little about his life, but he was a major participant in a tradition which emphasized ethics, meditation, devotion and compassionate action as being inseparable from the cultivation of wisdom. To see him just as a thinker is to misread Buddhism and to produce highly partial interpretations which, although they might be interesting to those who have a penchant for them, have little spiritual value.

What Buddhism most has to offer Western philosophy is the notion that ways of conceptualizing are intertwined with ways of being and although one *can* go about philosophy as if it were a purely intellectual exercise, there is little value in that — thought alone cannot apprehend reality. To truly understand how things really are one needs to bring about changes in the whole of one's psyche so that one apprehends the nature of things, not only with one's intellect, but with the whole of one's being. Thought can be a valuable element in spiritual practice. But it is only one element. Buddhism will really have engaged with Western philosophy when philosophers recognize that in order to really do philosophy one has to change oneself and in order to change oneself one has to do more than think.

This idea is not new to the Western philosophical tradition. The ancient Greco-Roman philosophers, from Plato through Marcus Aurelius to Plotinus and others, pursued wisdom (*sophia*) by engaging in a set of 'spiritual exercises', of which the sustained application of dialectical reasoning was only a part. There is a striking resemblance between some of these exercises and traditional Buddhist practice.[7] A genuine engagement between Buddhism and Western philosophy, rather than implying a break with tradition, might instead be seen as the opportunity for a return to an older, more vigorous and more thorough-going approach to the quest for truth.

Given the sophistication of the Buddhist analysis of the mind and its preoccupation with the eradication of suffering, it is only natural that strong similarities have come to be seen between Buddhism and the contemporary Western tradition of psychotherapy. Across the whole spectrum of psychoanalytic thinking there are resonances with the Buddhist tradition, be they Jungian resonances with Tantric symbolism or cognitive psychotherapy's resonance with the techniques of mindfulness training. There is even, in Core Process Therapy, a developing school of 'Buddhist psychotherapy', which makes use of the principle of conditionality.

Buddhism and psychotherapy, however, seek to alleviate human suffering to very different extents. Broadly speaking, the psychotherapeutic approach tends to be founded upon a sense of normative mental health. It aims to eradicate the more acute degrees of psychic dysfunction and to establish people in workable relationships with their environment. This is, very often, a valuable service. But the Buddhist approach is further reaching. It aims not for mental health but for Enlightenment — an altogether different proposition.

For Buddhism, all of life — even that of psychically well-adjusted, integrated human beings — is marked by suffering. So long as we are un-Enlightened, and continue to see the world in terms of subject and object, self and other, we will suffer and we will, out of ignorance, bring about suffering in others. The only way to overcome this is to gain

Enlightenment. Through the dedicated application of spiritual discipline, the subject–object dichotomy can be weakened and eventually transcended.

The Buddhist path begins with a recognition of the inevitability of suffering, a recognition which motivates one to tread the path to Enlightenment. This crucial focus, however, is sometimes lost sight of in Western Buddhist circles. As Buddhism and psychotherapy become closer acquainted with one another, there is an emerging trend towards a kind of psychotherapeutic Buddhism, where the impetus towards Enlightenment is replaced with the overriding impulse to simply come to terms with oneself, to feel better about oneself and the world. There is a kind of 'feelgood' approach emerging at the fringes of Western Buddhism which bypasses the idea that life is intrinsically unsatisfactory and focuses instead on ideas and practices which help one to experience a greater sense of being at ease in the world.

Some Buddhist practitioners experience persistent difficulties in their lives, patterns of behaviour which impel them to behave in ways which cause them and others to suffer and which they can begin to change if only they could become more aware of some of their deeper, unconscious impulses. In some cases the nature of these impulses can be revealed in the context of spiritual friendship. In others, it may take more skilled help, and psychotherapy might be useful. But the idea that one must first eradicate all of one's mental discomfort before one can begin to practise Buddhism is simply mistaken, as is the idea that the purpose of Buddhism itself is to make one feel a bit more comfortable with oneself and the world.

Buddhism has a great deal to offer the world of modern psychotherapy. It can also be completely absorbed into it.

For all the differences that exist between Buddhism and the contemporary worlds of art, science, philosophy and psychotherapy, however, its approach is closer in many ways to these than it is to the world of contemporary Western religion.

For the last 1,500 years monotheism has predominated within Western religious life so it is not surprising that most people in the West think that religion is about belief in God.

I am sometimes invited to attend different interfaith gatherings in Britain where I often hear well-meaning people say things like:

'Well of course we may belong to different religions but we all have something in common. Although he may present himself to us in different ways, we all really believe in the same God...'

'Ah, not quite, you see...' and I launch into my standard explanation. Buddhists don't believe in God.

It will be some time before most religious people in the West come to at least a basic understanding of Buddhist teachings and practices. Nonetheless, there have been a number of significant developments in this area, particularly in the area of Buddhist/Christian dialogue.

The modern age is the occasion of the first really meaningful encounter between Buddhism and Christianity. Until the nineteenth century, such contact as there was between them was almost insignificant. Buddhism and Christianity developed in mutual ignorance of one another and both tended to see themselves as religious absolutes, capable of explaining, within their own terms, all the spiritual facts of existence including, in theory at least, the teachings of other religions.

But Buddhism and Christianity have now been brought face to face. They are being forced to recognize one another as separate spiritual universes. Christianity can no longer dismiss Buddhism as a mere ethical system, or a form of natural mysticism and Buddhism cannot dismiss Christianity with a benign comment on the inadequacies of theism. From now on they have to take one another more seriously than that, and in order to do so they have to begin to communicate.[8]

The process of trying to establish a real dialogue, a genuine communication between Buddhism and Christianity is fraught with difficulty. Buddhism can share the language of conditionality with the arts, with science, philosophy and psychotherapy. But Christianity speaks a very different language. Buddhism and Christianity both have highly developed languages, but they are founded upon very different experiences and concepts. One cannot easily, if at all, directly translate from one to the other. Nonetheless, the two worlds are now engaged in discourse with one another — discourse of very different qualities.

One group of people who have shown a great interest in Buddhism of late are those post-Christians who, whilst not yet altogether ready to leave the Christian fold, feel the need to redefine God in terms more acceptable to their modern (and postmodern) sensibilities. One such grouping, the Sea of Faith Network[9], is strongly influenced by the work of the Cambridge theologian Don Cupitt. Religion, they insist, is a human, not a divine, construct and although there is no settled meaning given between them to the term 'God', they all tend to agree at least that 'realist' descriptions of him, as an embodied agent at work in the universe, are wholly inadequate.

Given these beliefs, it isn't surprising to know that Cupitt has called for a kind of Buddhist Christianity — a new kind of hybrid religion founded in the best of both traditions. Like the philosophers I discussed earlier, however, Cupitt misreads Buddhism by treating it as if it were making a number of merely philosophical propositions rather than ascribing a transformative course of spiritual training with a salvific goal.

The inability to let go of the thinking faculty leads Cupitt to a kind of entrapment within language. He sees the Mahayana Buddhist tradition as 'in a certain sense admirably non-realist', but 'although it has been aware of the opacity of language, it still seems in the end to try to go beyond language. In quiet seated meditation we divest ourselves of all vocabulary and let Impermanence presence itself in us, and this is It... it is being claimed in language that a certain fullness of Presence is attainable beyond language that is not attainable in language'. And this he cannot accept.[10]

There is, according to Cupitt (or at least Cupitt in 1992) 'nothing outside the text'. What cannot be said cannot be experienced. With this interesting twist on traditional Judaeo-Christian 'textual fundamentalism', Buddhism and Don Cupitt part company. Cupitt's attempt to synthesize Buddhism and Christianity is intellectually intriguing but, from the Buddhist perspective at least, it fails. And the reasons for this failure are interesting because they cast useful light on the true nature of inter-religious dialogue.

An effective synthesis can only come about over time and as a result of prolonged dialogue and interaction. It can't be achieved at a purely conceptual level. True dialogue, however, can only take place when committed, experienced practitioners of Buddhism and Christianity come together to try somehow to explain the nature of their different experiences to one another.

This kind of approach to Buddhist/Christian dialogue emerges from the work of Masao Abe, a Japanese Buddhist who teaches and writes on comparative religion. His book *Buddhism and Interfaith Dialogue*[11], contains an exemplary account of constructive engagement.

Abe enters into a public discussion with Paul Knitter, a prominent liberation theologian who is also well-versed in Zen Buddhism. Contrasting his experience of studying and meditating in Japan with his time working as a Christian social activist in El Salvador, Knitter considers the traditional Christian distinctions between contemplation and action, prayer and work. In Buddhism, he concludes 'You cannot change the world unless you sit', whereas in Christianity 'You cannot sit unless you change the world'. Wisdom, he concludes, comes before compassion in Buddhism. And so, without making the overtly biased judgements of earlier theologians, the old critique of Buddhist social passivity emerges.

Abe responds by pointing out that it is misleading to understand Buddhism merely as a preference for contemplation prior to action in the sense that one literally comes before the other. Rather, the two are intrinsically intertwined. The ideal Buddhist does not seek Enlightenment for himself alone, but continually returns to the world to aid living beings. One does not first sit and then engage with the world. Sitting and engagement go hand in hand. The tradition emphasizes 'Walking is Zen, sitting is Zen, whether talking or remaining silent, whether moving or standing quiet, the Essence itself is ever at ease: Even when greeted with swords and spears, it never loses its quiet way.' What is essential for Zen meditation is not physical sitting but a well-composed quiet mind under any circumstances.

Why, Knitter asks, are Buddhists apparently reluctant to associate the experience of the Formless Self with God? Because, Abe replies, the otherness of a personal God necessarily implies that one treats the Ultimate as an object, separate from oneself. This is not acceptable to Buddhism where the central issue is to awaken to one's True Self.

And so the discussion runs on, casting as much light on difference as on similarity. Carried out by people who understand their own traditions and who are really willing to listen to one another, a genuine dialogue between Buddhism and Christianity illuminates both.

Dialogue is vital. Premature conflation, however, just leads to woolliness and confusion. Thich Nhat Hanh, for example, hasn't helped the cause of Buddhist/Christian dialogue with his latest book *Living Buddha, Living Christ*.

Dan Wakefield, the book's reviewer, writes in *Tricycle* magazine:

I am no theologian, nor am I given to 'academic niceties', but as a Christian layperson I could not help wondering at some of the seemingly casual and questionable interpretations of Living Buddha, Living Christ.[12]

'I do not think there is that much difference between most Christians and most Buddhists.' Nhat Hanh tells us 'Most of the boundaries we have created between our two traditions are artificial. Truth has no boundaries. Our differences may be mostly differences of emphasis.'

His attempt to bolster this belief leads to such vague statements as 'Taking refuge in the Three Jewels is the foundation of every Buddhist practice. Taking refuge in the Trinity is at the foundation of every Christian practice.' Except for the fact that there are three of each, there is little comparison between the Buddha, Dharma and Sangha, and The Father, Son and Holy Ghost. Indeed, the very idea of the Trinity refutes Nhat Hanh's sweeping statement that Christians understand that God cannot be experienced through concepts.

In trying to draw Buddhism and Christianity closer together Nhat Hanh presents a misleading picture of both, and rather than furthering the cause of mutual understanding, actually makes genuine dialogue more difficult.

Over time, there is no doubt that Buddhism and Christianity will come to influence one another in the West. Perhaps, over a long period of time, a new kind of synthesis will emerge from the encounter. But that synthesis cannot be rushed and it certainly can't be achieved by blurring crucial differences, as in the case of Nhat Hanh, or by simply pushing abstract concepts together, as does Don Cupitt.

The interaction between Buddhism and Western culture, of course, is not confined to the rarefied worlds of art-criticism, science, philosophy, psychotherapy and theology. It takes place in the media as well and wherever Westerners encounter the Buddhist teachings.

Buddhism is experiencing a wave of media attention in the 1990s. From Hollywood we have had Bertolucci's *Little Buddha* and we are about to have Martin Scorsese's version of the Dalai Lama's autobiography *Freedom in Exile* and Robert Bolt's life of the Buddha. Media stars proclaim their Buddhist allegiance in interviews and the press recently followed Richard Gere to

Nepal, whence they fed back to the West perplexing pictures of his and Cindy Crawford's attendance at a lengthy public tantric initiation carried out by the Dalai Lama. The same Dalai Lama who recently guest-edited the Paris edition of *Vogue* (which showed clinging maroon dresses 'inspired' by Tibetan monks robes). Buddhism has become quite remarkably *chic*.[13]

According to a recent feature in the US fashion magazine *Harpers Bazaar*, 'Buddhism, or at least the Buddhist outlook on man and the universe is rapidly becoming the universally accepted world-view.' If only that were so. For similarities can obscure differences and it is where Buddhism *differs* from modern opinion, especially in the areas of ethics and lifestyle, that it has most to contribute.

In *Harpers and Queen* photographer Koo Stark described her discovery of Buddhism on a recent trip to Nepal. 'Suddenly in the middle of the most beautiful nowhere there rose the majestic silhouette of a Tibetan Buddhist monastery. A majestic sight.' Returning home, she found 'you don't have to renounce anything to become a Buddhist, you simply incorporate it into your daily life.' As *Harpers Bazaar* put it: 'You may be able to keep your job... wear Chanel... eat chocolate... and still be enlightened.'

The consumer society has a way of dealing with subversive challenges. It co-opts them, sanitises them, makes them its own and then, when they are no longer a threat and no longer interesting, discards them.

Buddhism began to die out in India during the 12th and 13th centuries. This was largely the result of various Muslim invasions, carried out by different Turkish peoples from Central Asia, but there were also several subsidiary causes which Western Buddhists would do well to note.

By the 12th century Indian Buddhism had largely become a religion of scholastic, monastic, specialists occupying grand university-monasteries. Hinduism, meanwhile, which remained based in the villages and maintained close links with the general populace, had come in certain respects to resemble Buddhism more closely. Popular Hindu philosopher-teachers, although hostile to Buddhism in many respects, often appropriated Buddhist philosophical concepts and Buddhist lay-practice came increasingly to resemble Hindu popular culture.

The Muslim invaders sacked and destroyed the monasteries. Their historians record that, standing out as they did on the northern Indian plains, the great universities were mistaken for fortresses. The occupants were murdered, their libraries destroyed, before anyone had time to explain matters. The monastic institutions, for all their aloofness, had long functioned as the guardians of Buddhist doctrinal and methodological purity. Once they were destroyed the means of distinguishing between what was Buddhist and what was Hindu was also lost and Buddhism was soon absorbed into popular culture, effectively disappearing from its country of origin.

Buddhism can change popular culture but it can also be absorbed and destroyed by it.

In an interview with Helen Tworkov, the editor of *Tricycle* magazine, Roshi Philip Kapleau, founder of the Rochester Zen Center in New York, sounds a crucial warning.

Helen Tworkov: Recently I was at a meeting in Santa Fe with a mix of Buddhists from all different traditions, and someone said that we got so caught up in identifying corruption – money, sex, power – that we lost sight of the real corruption in Buddhism, which is the way teachings are being altered to make them palatable to an American Sangha.

Kapleau Roshi: I fully agree. That is, if you mean making the practices easier or less disciplined. Then there are other corruptions as well, such as the appropriation of fundamental elements of Zen training by psychotherapists who give them a psychological twist. Or you find therapists teaching their patients meditation and equating it with spiritual liberation. Another threat to the integrity of Zen, and in many ways the most bizarre, is that of Zen teachers sanctioning Catholic priests and nuns as well as rabbis and ministers to teach Zen... [14]

Over the course of the current century Buddhism has been under attack, almost throughout Asia. In Tibet, China, Mongolia, Vietnam, Laos and Cambodia Buddhist communities have suffered horrifying depredations. Never before in human history has any major religion diminished so rapidly in size and influence. Indeed, three or four well-placed revolutions would more or less eliminate traditional Buddhism altogether[15]. Even in those Buddhist countries which have not suffered under Communism, like Thailand and Japan, consumerism is eroding the traditional values upon which a Buddhist way of life was based. The only bright spots in this otherwise gloomy picture are India, where a Buddhist revival is underway, and the West, where Buddhism is gradually taking root in the hearts and minds of tens, perhaps even hundreds of thousands of devoted practitioners.

In coming to the West, the Buddhist teachings have encountered what is probably their greatest ever challenge. Can they really help to transform a culture as large, as proud, as rich, powerful, confused and fragmented as our own? I believe they can. Buddhism has the capacity to ignite a cultural and spiritual renaissance in the West. But it can do so only if it remains Buddhism. For that to happen, Westerners must strive to understand and practise it on *its* terms, not on theirs.

People speak of the need to integrate Buddhism into Western society. But that assumes, somehow, that Western society will remain unchanged by the encounter. If that happens then Buddhism will simply be absorbed and subsumed, co-opted as yet another interesting element within a pervasive consumer culture. If Buddhism is to help to bring about radical changes in the world we live in, then rather than integrating Buddhism into Western society what we really have to do is to integrate Western society into Buddhism, and that is a far more radical, far more challenging task.

---

1. Stephen Batchelor, *The Awakening of the West: the Encounter of Buddhism and Western Culture*, Aquarian, 1994.

2. Harold Bloom, *The Western Canon*, Papermac, 1994.

3. Joanna Macy, *Mutual Causality and General Systems Theory: the Dharma of Natural Systems*, SUNY, 1991.

4. ibid.

5. Joanna Macy, *World as Lover, World as Self*, Rider, 1993.

6. Andrew Tuck, *Comparative Philosophy and the Philosophy of Scholarship: on the Western Interpretation of Nagarjuna*, Oxford University Press, 1990.

7. Pierre Hadot, *Philosophy as a Way of Life*, ed. Arnold I. Davidson, Blackwell, 1995.

8. Sangharakshita, 'Dialogue Between Buddhism and Christianity', in *The Priceless Jewel*, Windhorse, 1993.

9. The Sea of Faith Network is not exclusively Christian, but Christianity is its predominant preoccupation.

10. Don Cupitt, *The Time Being*, SCM Press, 1992.

11. Masao Abe, *Buddhism and Interfaith Dialogue*, edited by Steven Heine, Macmillan Press Ltd., 1995.

12. *Tricycle: the Buddhist Review*, Winter 1995.

13. See 'The Rise of Dharma Chic', Vishvapani, in *Golden Drum No. 33*, July 1994, Windhorse Publications.

14. *Tricycle: the Buddhist Review*, Summer 1993.

15. Stephen Batchelor, *Tricycle: the Buddhist Review*, Winter 1995.